# DESPERATE MEN AND WOMEN

# DESPERATE MEN AND WOMEN :

## Ten Dalit Short Stories from India

**B. RANGRAO**

KALPAZ

ISBN : 978-81-7835-998-4

₹ 450

First Published 2013

*Published by*

**Kalpaz Publications**
C-30, Satyawati Nagar,
Delhi-110052
Ph. : 9212142040
E-mail: kalpaz@hotmail.com

*Laser Typesetting* : Rudra Computer Graphics, Delhi
*Printed at* : G. Print Process, Delhi

**Cataloging in Publication Data—DK**
Courtesy: D.K. Agencies (P) Ltd. <docinfo@dkagencies.com>

**Rangrao, B.**
**Desperate Men and Women : Ten Dalit Short Stories from India** / B. Rangrao
p. cm.
Short stories.
Includes index.
Contents: Childbirth — Death of a rich man — Farewell — When the Sun God refused to set — And quiet flowed the purnamai- — A tale told by a scavenger — Cobbler, cobbler mend my shoe — Loneliness of an ex-soldier — Kulatha Rangan — Confessions of a graveyard keeper.

ISBN 9788178359984

1. Dalits—India—Fiction. 2. Short stories, Indic (English). I.Title.

DDC 823.92 23

# Contents

# Preface

***Desperate Men and Women***, the title of this book, with the subtitle that follows it, is self-explanatory. Political freedom brought little cheers to a community which had led the life of perpetual servility under the rigid caste system in India. Caste is understood as *jat* or *jati* in Indian languages which literally means *to go* or *to leave* but, ironically, caste never went away from the Indian mindset even though it was abolished legally by the constitution makers. And the victims of the caste system continued to suffer as their forefathers did. The characters in the stories that follow are the evidence. They are the imaginary creations, yet speak of the social reality that prevails everywhere in India. They are all the citizens of a free nation, and yet, freedom eschews them like a truant school boy who finds learning uninteresting.

The stories, however, are the literary efforts of my creative sensibility I have sustained throughout the last four decades or so. They are not social documents, nor do they have political connotations, rather projections of the social reality perceived by a creative mind which has itself undergone and experienced much that is portrayed in the stories. Dalit creative sensibility has been adequately expressed through regional languages in India; in English, however, only a few books can claim to have dealt with it thoroughly. Caste is the major underlying factor of the Dalit experience. Other factors like class, gender, race or creed deviate the focus from the main issue and lead it towards another form of essentialism, which, in turn, leaves the Indian social reality half-perceived. Creativity, of course, results out of personal experience and its understanding, and cannot be a matter of comparison. Therefore, no claim can be laid toward superiority of these stories in English, but they are basically *Dalit* in essence, that is confirmed.

The stories in the book are set in the various regions in India. Not that I have lived in these regions really, but the Dalit experience with its pangs of being outcaste does not differ fundamentally; rather, results in the similar narrative, oral or written. After all, isn't untouchability a national stigma that lingers in the psychic region of an average Indian? The stories, it is hoped, do come up to the expectations of readers in India and abroad and help enhance Dalit creativity in English.

**B. Rangrao**

# Acknowledgement

I acknowledge, with a sense of deep gratitude, the cooperation rendered by Kalpaz Publications by telling me that these stories are highly readable and reveal an unknown facet of social reality in India, and, subsequently, taking them up for publication.

**B. Rangrao**

# Introduction

Expression of Dalit sensibility through literary efforts is not a new phenomenon. What has been generally termed as folklore is, in fact, the artistic expression of men and women who had no access to the foundational world order. Dalit is the term in the Indian context which refers to these men and women who were once untouchable and who regaled in self-satisfying creativity. They were a part of the masses set aside against the class. Therefore, their voices were never audible to the set canons. The canonical norms evoked the universal spirit that occluded these men and women and affirmed certain standards which catered to their own needs. Philosophies and ethical codes failed to encompass within their range the inequality and injustice that lay afoot in the social structure. They were concerned with the universe that consisted of the elite and the powerful. They came out with interpretation of the universe that suited their own purpose, offered canons for artistic pursuits, determined the nature of relationship between man and woman, slave and master, and among the innumerable castes that thronged the soil. They created a small pond of intellectual luxuries and called it classics. They produced language drawing words and signs from their own surroundings which was supported by the coterie of zombies. They denied the status of language to what others spoke and affirmed that their language alone is capable of the universal interpretation. Their language alone was suitable for artistic creativity and for evoking the divine spirit. Their language alone was said to be the proper means of communication in civilized society. The supremacy of certain linguistic norms was thus established over others and unjustly sanctioned. These norms were later confirmed by law and religion. This came to be called culture and civilization.

The history of enlightenment and modernity progressed on this line of thinking. This was true not only of India but of every other civilization in the world. The Dalit condition was not the only outcome of the canonical culture. It produced several such conditions like slavery, racism, sexism etc. While enlightenment and modernity insisted on excellence, it cast a blind eye to the miseries, wretchedness, squalor, poverty and a set of inhuman practices carried out in the name of law and religion. It upheld social discrimination and affirmed the notion *the best and the rest*. The two historical phases, namely enlightenment and modernity, produced thinkers and philosophers whose thinking has no relevance to the restless masses of the day. Namdeo Dhasal, a prominent Dalit poet in Marathi, puts it in one of his poems—

*Plato, Einstein, Archimedes*
*Socrates, Marx, Ashok, Hitlar-Bitlar, Camus,*
*Sartre, Kafka, Baudelaire, Rambo, Ezra pound,*
*Hopkins, Goethe, Dostoyevsky, Mykoevsky, Maxim Gorky,*
*Edison-Medison, Kalidas, Tukaram, Homer, Vyas, Valmiki,—*
*Throw them away into the gutter man hole.*

Literature of the Dalits in India, or the Dalit literary movement, as it has been aptly called, is a part of that global phenomenon, which, in historical sense, has been termed as postmodernism. Modernism, with its association with the classical values like reason and universality, often tends to ignore the difference and assumes the totalitarian stance. It never had a sense of social obligation. Postmodernism, on the other hand, offers scope for pluralism and diversity. It addresses itself to the issues of gender, race and, in the Indian context, caste. Like other neglected social groups elsewhere in the world, the Dalits in India distrust the universal philosophies as repressive. They share the postmodernist desire to challenge the repressive power of culturally dominant grand narrative and are interested in creating their own little narratives with their own voice and stories heard. The ten Dalit short stories in this book raise the voices of desperate men and women who are the victims of the repressive social dominance. While most of the characters in the stories, the readers will realize, suffer mutely, others break away from the traditional norms.

Literature today is marked for technical innovations; something which modernist sensibility had pioneered during 1920s. Indian English writing flirted with these innovations for quite sometimes. The early efforts by fiction writers in Indian English were modeled on the British masters like E.M. Forster. James Joyce, Graham Greene and others. After the fall of Empire and the two world wars there was a major shift in socio-cultural situation resulting ultimately into different literary modes and techniques. Indian English writing responded to it promptly and, as the time progressed, evolved its own literary techniques relying much upon the native myths and oral tradition. Contemporary Indian English fiction stands apart for its resistance to the Euro-centric norms and for evocating the native spirit. Salman Rushdie and his followers have drawn the lines that are being followed by others for creativity.

*Desperate Men and Women* does attempt, to a certain extent, technical novelty; these stories, however, are to be read not for technicalities but for their boldness of theme and subject matter. Here is an attempt to subvert literary canons by laying open the world of men and women whose once peripheral experiences occupy the centre stage today.

**RB**

# 1

# Childbirth

Rakhma knew that her days were up. She will have to deliver the baby any moment, now that it was well over nine months since she had conceived. But she could not afford to stay at home while her workmates go to work and earn the wages. This would mean to let her family starve—her lazy husband and two wayward children. Her husband did not have a sense of family obligation and spent most of his time at home doing nothing. His favorite hobby was smoking *bidis* coupled with eating two meals a day at the cost of his wife's meager earning. Rakhma desired her two sons—eight and five years of age respectively—should go to school like the children in neighborhood. But she did not have the resources to buy them books and study material. There were no facilities offered to the poor by the government then as they are being offered today. The boys, therefore, roamed in the village lanes and helped their mother occasionally. Rakhma was always anxious about their future.

It was the rainy season and the sky was strewn with clouds that might cause downpour of rain. Presently, however, there was no threat to working conditions in the agriculture fields. Therefore, men and women prepared themselves for work.

"Wait, O Shanta", Rakhma yelled out at a woman who had just gone by, "wait for a while and I will join you soon".

"Why do you want to come, Rakhma", the woman replied, "you know well enough that your days are up and—"

"It's necessary", Rakhma cut her short and said- "otherwise my children will starve tonight. You know that my husband is good only for eating. He doesn't go to work. How will I feed my children if I stay back home?"

Shanta had no answer. She realised the truth in what Rakhma said. At the same time she was concerned with Rakhma's plight—her protruding belly carrying fully developed *embryo* likely to be born any moment, her inability to walk properly and the occasional pain she had been experiencing for almost two days now. She, however, was helpless about it and agreed to take Rakhma along with her.

A couple of women joined them as they went ahead through the lane. Finally, a group of about six women marched towards a field where they were supposed to weed out the grass from the cultivated land. An old man, probably, the owner of the field, followed them. He would supervise the work to be carried out by the women. The group reached the field, a piece of well cultivated land of about ten acres. The cotton seeds sown a month ago or so, had sprouted nicely. The crop, however, was surrounded by unwanted grass to be weeded out. This is a part of usual practice of farming in Indian villages.

The man had allotted rows of crop to be attended to. The women set themselves to work. They adapted themselves to the work at hand. While their hands skillfully removed the unwanted grass, their mouths, at the same time, began to mutter. Each one of them had a tale to narrate. All of them belonged to the caste, once untouchable, now lost in the mist of political humbug. Each one of them had received humiliation, some time or other, at the hands of caste men and beating from their own. They were women and untouchable. The tales they narrated had common thread of misery, poverty and ignorance. One of them had this to offer—

"My husband came drunk last night, the home-brewed liquor from the *lala*'s shop, and beat me. He even raised his hand against my married daughter who has come to visit us from her in-laws house yesterday because she objected to his unruly behavior."

The other one narrated thus—"The *patwari l*ooked straight at me the other day when I was adjusting my *pallu*. There was something lecherous in his eyes—yes, there certainly was."

Here is yet another story—

"As if it happened yesterday—I remember it so vividly", said a woman. "I was just married then and had come to live with my in-laws. My mother-in-law, a woman of about forty, had good looks. Though not very fair, rather dark complexioned, she stood out among many women of our community even at that age. My father-in–law worked as a labourer at the *Patil's* farm. He even worked as a domestic servant sometimes.The *Patil* used to visit our house and always enquired about our wellbeing. He was particularly friendly with my mother-in-law. We were happy because he would always help when in need. He would send sweets on festival days like *Diwali, Holi* etc.

"On a rainy day, when work came to a standstill, we all went to the temple to listen to *Pandav Pratap*, all except my mother-in-law, who preferred to stay back home and rest. The *Patil,* who was already present there, enquired about his *vahini* – that was my mother-in-law. On learning that she was alone at home, he quietly disappeared from the crowd. He went to our house and found the woman alone lying leisurely on a cot. The man forced himself into my mother-in-law. He raped her and came out quietly. When we returned home we found my mother-in-law crying desperately, her clothes torn and hair scattered. She narrated the incident to her husband. My father-in-law got mad with anger. He picked up an axe in the corner, went to the *Patil's* house, got hold of him and chopped him into pieces. He was arrested the next day, tried and was sent to prison for ten years. He never repented the deed through the rest of his life. My mother-in-law waited for her husband but died before he was released."

Rakhma listened to the tales narrated by her companions, and, at the same time, moved smoothly across the rows. Her agility and capacity to work even at that stage of pregnancy was amazing. She suddenly became aware of her condition as a pang of pain shot up in her belly. She knew what it was and realised that endurance will hold no longer now. She called out to Shanta—"O mai," they often called out each other by assumed relations, "the time has come, the time for me to go back home. Tell him the reason why I have to leave work in the middle."

Saying so Rakhma stood up. She collected the bits she had brought with her and began to walk towards home. She wondered where her husband would be, whether he would be of some help at this hour of need. She also thought of her sons, the urchins wandering through the lanes of village.

The stray clouds in the sky had consolidated themselves and looked quite intimidating. A possibility of heavy rain appeared quite close.

Rakhma reached home to find it deserted. Her husband, who would lie idly smoking in the corner, was absent. Her sons nowhere to be seen. Someone should call the woman in the village who attends childbirths—*dai* as she is generally known. There was no one in sight. 'What do I do?' Rakhma said to herself. Pain spurned in the abdomen turning the woman helpless. As it became unbearable she lied down on the ground. Her lower body was wreathing with pain. Screams spurted out of her mouth but she was able to suppress them. Now, there was a movement inside the uterus. Rakhma knew what to do. She untied the cloth around her waist and put it aside. She then parted her thighs and began to push. Not many efforts were needed. The baby came tumbling down in a pool of blood and began to cry. Rakhma felt relieved as the pain abated. She stretched her hand out to a sickle lying nearby, placed herself in sitting position and cut the baby's umbilical cord. She lifted the baby, wiped it with the cloth and held it close to her breast. The baby began to suck the nipple instinctively.

Childbirth leaves both mother and the baby hungry. While the baby brings it down to the earth, mother's hunger is evoked by the space in the stomach left by the newborn. This hunger is so strong that animals are often said to eat up their own progenies. Mother scorpion is killed immediately, unable to withstand the pangs of hunger. God has created hunger, but the creator has failed to produce means to pacify it. Something similar happened in the case of Rakhma.

While it started raining outside Rakhma experienced a big vacuum inside her, at a place where she bore the baby. This vacuum demanded to be filled in immediately. That was hunger at its highest intensity. She looked around. There were a few earthen pots and she knew that they contained nothing, not even a particle of food. She put the baby down, wrapped herself with the threadbare cloth that left half of her body uncovered. She came out of the house. Rain poured down quietly. Rakhma seemed unaware of it. The stains of blood on her thighs showed that she was bleeding profusely. There was a small grocery shop at a distance. Rakhma headed towards it.

She walked up slowly, maintaining balance as she felt reeling through dizziness, also to protect herself from the slipperiness that the rain had produced. She must eat something immediately, otherwise this hunger will tear her apart. She speeded up a little. The grocery shops in Indian villages form a part of living apartment and are run by the family members alternately. When Rakhma reached the shop there was no one at the counter. The owner seemed to have gone inside to eat or to enjoy siesta. Items of daily consumption like jiggery, salt, edible oil etc. lay open. Rakhma wanted to request the shopkeeper to give her something on credit. She will pay for it later. But whom to tell? She thought. Her eyes fell on a bag filled with ground nuts. As she picked up a handful of ground nuts someone yelled at her from inside—"hey, keep the stuff, you thief. How dare you....." It was the woman in the house who suspected a trespasser. She knew Rakhma very well. She also knew that Rakhma was pregnant. But she could not recognise Rakhma in that strange appearance—in a single torn piece of cloth, dripping, hair stuck around the neck and bleeding. What happened to her? Why is she in that horrible condition, the woman wondered?

Rakhma had turned back by now and started running towards home. The thought of her baby lying alone and unprotected brought her back to herself. She held the ground nuts in her fist but forgot to put them in mouth. Hunger seemed to have disappeared. By the time she reached home she was exhausted totally. She crossed the threshold and before she could reach out to her baby, collapsed. She lay motionless in a pool of blood, unaware of the life of her own, of the baby she had begotten. Rain had gathered momentum outside and began to fall fiercely.

# 2

# Death of a Rich Man

"Satyawan Tryambak Meshram", teacher called out the name. There was no response. Boys and girls in the class turned their heads to see if Satyawan was present. He was nowhere to be seen.

"*No guruji*", someone clarified, "Sattya has not come even today".

Teacher got annoyed. 'How will he pass the examination and go to the next class', he said to himself. 'Why don't his parents take proper care of the boy and send him to school?'

At that precise hour, Satyawan Tryambak Meshram, better known as Sattya, was enjoying the cool water of the river-swimming, diving and jumping down from the cliffs atop into the river water. He was not alone. Several boys in the locality, who were his constant companions, were engaged in the act. Sattya was seven years of age, weak and fragile, but swift enough to pose challenge to his friends in their local games. He was recently enrolled in school but was never interested in learning. He could never understand why three into four becomes twelve and not something else. He always made mistakes and was eventually punished by the teacher.

Sattya's father was a member of a band party which played music at weddings. When there were no marriages around he was without work. His mother earned a little but her earning was meager and never enough to meet the expenses. They had to look after two children other than Sattya, who were five and three years old. Therefore, Sattya's father expected that his son, whom he had enrolled in school, should also work in spare time and help the family. Sattya never fulfilled his father's expectations. He avoided school as much as possible, and when there was some work at hand he avoided that too. He whiled away time with other boys from his community who played truant and, like Sattya, were termed as lazy and useless by their parents. No wonder, then, that Sattya's father was always cross with him and scolded the boy whenever he could.

The river that flowed by the village contained plenty of water. It sustained the quiet village life even in the smarting heat of summer. The river was a symbol of liveliness where every activity explained the meaning of life in Indian villages. It washed the newborn of its blood-smeared skin, it offered enormous scope to young men and women for their youthful activities. It also generously adopted within itself the old folk who wished to breath their last watching the river flow. The boys were often found either swimming in the river, or playing in its sand. They would notice burial of the dead on the bank of river, or cremation of the dead bodies. The river bank was used as graveyards separately by the two communities. The lower castes would bury their dead while the higher castes would cremate them. The boys would visit the graveyard after the funeral rites got over because they would find some coins scattered around the grave and at a place where dead bodies were cremated. Death of a rich man would earn them some money as the affluent show their generosity more in death than in life.

It was a small village divided by castes and communities. The people knew each other despite the caste barriers. They also kept information about the slightest event that took place. So, when *seth* Jhabarmal—who was well over eighty years of age—fell seriously ill, the news spread like wild fire. *Seth* Jhabarmal was a rich *marwadi* whose forefathers had migrated from Rajasthan and settled down here. In fact, when the *marwadis* came down they did not bring anything with them except a *dhoti* and *lota*- a small metal pitcher. How they amassed wealth disproportionately is a mystery.

*Seth* Jhabarmal was bed-ridden for almost six months. Several doctors were called, *ayurvedic* treatment applied but there was no improvement in his health. It deteriorated from day to day. He was finally placed down the *charpai* which was a sure sign of fast approaching death. The inevitable happened. The *seth* passed away the next day. Each one forwarded the information to another. The entire village came to know that the *seth* was no more. *Seth* Jhabarmal was a nice man, not precisely popular in today's sense, but people thought well of him. He was liberal towards women, towards young women in particular. His demise, therefore, saddened the vicinity.

An alarm bell rang through the minds of Sattya and his friends. They gathered near seth Jhabarmal's big mansion. It was a hugh sprawling construction making it difficult to locate the main door. Sattya and his friends could make it out by the crowd that had gathered there. They walked to the crowd and learnt that the *seth*'s dead body would be taken to the graveyard for cremation after all the relatives arrive. The *seth*'s granddaughter, who was married last year, is on the way. The *seth* was very much fond of this girl, therefore, his body cannot be taken away unless she has his last *darshan*.

People kept coming in and out. All the preparations were made to carry the *seth*'s body to the graveyard. The relatives had also arrived except the granddaughter who was expected any moment. The boys had to wait. It was a long, an unbearable wait. Finally, a bullock cart with an arched cloth covering stopped at the door. A young woman stepped out of it. She was followed by a man and two elderly women. The boys at a distance heaved a sigh of relief. However, they were not sure whether she was the same granddaughter of the *seth* who was married last year and whom they had seen so closely as a bride. They also wondered if she was the same woman whose arrival was awaited so eagerly.

"She is not the same, she looks different", one of the boys said.

"She is the same", another argued.

"Can't be sure. She has bigger breasts. She did not have so big last year", the first one doubted.

"It happens after marriage, you idiot, husbands make it so", the retort.

"How do you know?"………

A sudden commotion diverted the boys' attention. Women's wailing voice prevailed. They all looked ahead intently. A man with an earthen bowl containing ambers that emanated smoke came out. He was followed by four men carrying the ladder. *Seth* Jhabarmal's dead body was taken to the graveyard for cremation. The boys took positions like jackals on the prowl. This was an occasion to earn a few coins and prove their worth to their parents who considered them as worthless. They would not let it go.

It is customary among the affluent Hindus to hurl one rupee coins, sometimes of greater value, over the dead bodies while they are being carried to the graveyard. It is a mark of paying homage to the dead. For the poor, it is an opportunity to collect the leftover, out of the dead, though. Men followed the ladder bearers. Several others joined them so that a long procession began to move slowly on the road. The boys divided themselves into two groups and took sides -right and left. Sonorous noise of *Ram nam satya hai* floated in the air. It continued for some time. A handful of coins were hurled across the corpse. The unfailing eyes of the boys noticed them. They did not have patience to wait till the coins fell on the ground and scrambled for the coins trying to catch them in the air. The intrusion in the procession annoyed the men who tried to shoo them away. The men knew that these boys from the low castes are perpetual nuisance, but are harmless, nevertheless. Besides, the coins hurled across the corpse were meant for the poor who would pray for the dead and bless his soul. Therefore, the annoyance they felt would give way to tolerance. Then they would chant monotonously—*Ram nam satya hai...* Coins were hurled once again across the corpse and the boys once again leapt towards them like hungry leopards.

The procession was moving towards the graveyard which now had come within the sight. The river, with usual flurries of activities on its bank, flowed quietly. Most of the boys had their catches. Sattya had none. 'Shall I have to go without any?' He asked himself, 'How shall I show face to my father? If I fail and go home without the catch father will surely beat me up.' He shuddered at the thought of beating. But all is not lost, he told himself again, 'Coins are still being hurled. I shall make another effort, the last and the best'....Sound of the coins brought him back to himself. He caught sight of the coins flung in the air, and, like the baby *Hanuman* leaping towards the rising sun, leapt towards the coins. He missed them and fell on the ground like a hugh pumpkin dropped down. This disarrayed the procession for a while. The men cursed the boy, abused and called him names. They, however, soon resumed their positions and moved ahead to cremate their dead trampling upon the limbs of the boy. The funeral procession of *Seth* Jhabarmal reached the graveyard while Sattya's motionless body lay unattended in the street. The chanting sound in chorus was heard once again—*Ram nam satya hai...Ram nam satya hai...*

# 3

# Farewell

It was a small village in the remote Indian countryside surrounded by thick forest on one side and by hillocks on the other. At the daybreak when the sun rose slowly behind the hillocks the entire horizon appeared brightly lit as if in a painting by Ravi Varma. The birds left their nests in search of food and cattle were let free to drink at the river and to graze. The entire village came alive after the peaceful night. Young girls were seen rushing towards the river with pitchers on the heads while elderly men and women engaged themselves in preparations for the day's work. As the day progressed and the sun became sober in the afternoon the familiar calm prevailed till the evening when the villagers would interact and bustle in the narrow dusty lanes.

Farming was the main source of income for the villagers. Land owners would grow crops like cotton, sorghum, pearl millet, corn, rice, wheat etc. The entire farming depended on the rain. The rain used to fall heavily during those days and the villagers used to reap good harvest.

Lakhan lived in this village with his family. He had a loving wife named Jamuna and two children. His old parents also lived with him. Jamuna helped her husband in running the household, took care of the children and in-laws who totally relied on her. Lakhan was a labourer who toiled hard to feed his folk. Jamuna would also join the working women and add to the family's scanty income. The children were not old enough to go to school, but Lakhan and Jamuna had already planned to send them to school when they reach that age.

Lakhan's parents had raised him amid hardships and poverty. They belonged to the caste considered as untouchable and suffered from all the evils of the caste system. Lakhan's father had worked as a bonded labourer to rich farmers and earned good will and reputation as a sincere and hardworking man. His ancestors belonged to this place and, though he has inherited from them nothing but a sense of being untouchable, always at the mercy of others, he revered their memory. He celebrated in his own small way the annual festival of *pitrumokshka amavashya* when all the Hindus remember their forefathers. He loved his parents too and would serve them as long as they live. He would enquire about their health as soon as he entered the house; children's welfare came next. Jamuna knew this and understood her husband's sentiments very well. Lakhan's parents were proud of their son and prayed to God for his long life and prosperity.

Independence brought little to the Indian village folk. Poverty and ignorance prevailed as they used to earlier. Health and hygiene remained a distant dream. So when an epidemic broke out in Lakhan's village people believed it as the divine wrath. There was an old shrine in the village. It was in dilapidated condition. It remained neglected for several years now. Even the idol of Goddess was missing. The village chief consulted the people and decided to restructure the temple and restore the idol immediately. Everyone was to contribute, either by paying a sum of rupees, or by offering physical labour. The epidemic had already taken a couple of lives and several others were sick when the work began. Lakhan's father was the latest victim of the deadly disease who passed away quietly one night. Lakhan was deeply aggrieved, so was Jamuna and other members of the family. Even those who were envious of the well knit family and its comfort, felt the sad demise of the old man. Lakhan made preparations for the last rites and extended consolation to others. Relatives were called, neighbours joined and the old man's dead body was taken out. Four men shouldering the ladder walked ahead and came in the main lane that led towards the graveyard. Others followed them. Suddenly, they were asked to stop. The village chief himself had come out with a few other castemen. He called out to Lakhan and asked him to divert the way as the temple being reconstructed is situated on this lane. If the dead body of an untouchable is carried through this lane the Goddess will disapprove of it and might cast severe afflictions on the entire village.

Lakhan was stunned by what he was told. The argument did not convince him. He belonged to this village as much as others did, and was concerned with the village welfare like all others. His father has served the village and offered his services to the Goddess herself by cleaning the temple, looking after its premises and attending it as a night watchman when he was young. Everyone knows it. How can the mother Goddess be so unkind as to get infuriated because his dead body is carried through the lane where her temple is to be rebuilt? She certainly knows the worth of the man—pure-hearted servant of the people and a total devotee of the Goddess herself. Besides, all his ancestors went to the graveyard by this lane. The lane itself is grateful to his ancestors for the services they had offered to the village. To take his father's dead body by some other lane will certainly hurt his father. His soul will not rest in peace. Lakhan decided to take his father's dead body to the graveyard according to the original plan.

"How dare you disobey the chief's order?" One of the chief's companions asked, "Are you bent on destroying the lives of us all?"

"Not at all," said Lakhan, "on the contrary, I wish to do everything for the village safety."

"Then turn the direction and take some other lane to reach the graveyard", the chief himself had commanded.

"Except this", said Lakhan politely, "I shall do everything except this. Allow us to proceed through the lane and I shall do everything you suggest."

"No", thundered the village chief, "this cannot be allowed. You will have to take different lane. This is the wish of the mother Goddess Herself."

Lakhan did not bow down to the chief's command. He asked his men to proceed further. The men walked ahead to the graveyard through the same lane, passing by the shrine, and buried the dead body on the bank of the river.

Lakhan was not brave precisely, but he had conviction. Besides, he loved his father beyond a trace of doubt. He knew the consequences of disobeying the chief, and was ready to face them in whatever manner they come. The thirteenth day of his father's death got over, all formalities completed. Everything seemed to be normal when, all of a sudden, one day, Jamuna returned home with her eyes downcast and saddened face. She was denied work and sent back by her workmates. Her mother-in-law was surprised to see her and asked—

"Why did you come back, Jamuna? What happened?"

"Nothing," Jamuna told her, "not feeling well, that's all."

She sat in a corner waiting for her husband to come. Lakhan came late, with a feeling of something gone amiss. He had strange experiences today, but could not make out what exactly it all was. As he entered the house he went straight away to the bed. Jamuna saw him entering and stood up to receive him but was surprised to see her husband's unusual behavior. She approached him slowly and saw him lying on the cot. She placed her hand on his forehead and asked—"What happened? Not feeling well?"

"Hmm..., Lakhan simply uttered.

"Shall I press your head a little", Jamuna asked.

"No, its all right," Lakhan felt irritated.

Jamuna could sense something uncomfortable. She recalled her own experiences of the day. In an attempt to pacify her husband she asked him—"Shall I serve the meal?"

"No", said Lakhan, "don't feel like eating".

"Are you going to sleep empty-stomach?"she asked.

"Leave me alone", said Lakhan with deep irritation, "Eat yourself and go to sleep".

Jamuna went to bed quietly. Her mother-in-law helped the children eat and herself ate a little. Lakhan and Jamuna slept without food. They had nightmares and were haunted by unknown fears. The day dawned upon the horizon slowly. Lakhan and Jamuna left their beds and engaged themselves with the work at hand.

The village chief finally had asserted his power. It was his personal ego and the sense of authority that was hurt by Lakhan's disobedience when he steered his father's funeral *yatra* despite the chief's refusal. The chief consulted his yeomen who hailed from his own caste and a few others who were convinced of Lakhan's foolhardiness. They decreed an order stating that Lakhan and his family members are excommunicated for all the purposes. Nobody from the village will have any interaction with Lakhan's family. Nobody will give them work, or allow them to buy from the shops. Lakhan's community men were likely to defy the order. They were threatened with dire consequences if they do not comply. Eventually they did.

Lakhan spent the day at home with his wife, doing nothing. His old mother gazed blankly at them alternately. She came to know the cause of her son's plight and was deeply agitated. She had known the chief's family since the day she had come to this village as a young bride. She knew how ruthless those people are. Therefore, she had no hopes for her son's retrieval. Lakhan, however, was unwilling to accept the decree. He decided to approach the chief and beg for justice. Begging was all that he could do. He had neither means nor support to challenge the chief's order. His courage and conviction were like weapons that have not been in use. They would hardly bring out any effect.

He could not dissuade Jamuna from accompanying him to the chief's court. They went together and found themselves facing the chief. The chief, as usual, was surrounded by his men. He was not surprised to see Lakhan approaching him with his wife, because he knew they would. He immediately assumed an authoritative stance and tried to appear as stern as he could. Lakhan greeted the chief with folded hands. So did Jamuna. The chief disregarded their greetings and looked at other direction. Lakhan was polite enough to attract the chief's attention when he spoke—

"Have mercy on my old mother and little children, who will die of hunger if you do not allow us freedom."

"Freedom?" the chief asked contemptuously, "which freedom do you talk about? You people never deserve freedom. You were born in perpetual slavery and will die in it as always."

"Please take back the excommunication order and let us live with whatever little we have", Lakhan pleaded.

"No", said the chief, "that is the punishment for the sin you have committed."

"Which sin do you refer to, sir?" asked Lakhan.

"Oh, I see," said the chief, "You don't remember now the act of your disobedience, when you took away your father's dead body from the front of Goddess temple despite our command. You have forgotten it, ah?"

"How can that be sin, sir?" enquired Lakhan."Was not my father a native of this village? Was he not a faithful servant of the people and of the Goddess herself ? How do you deny an honourable death to a man?"

"Honourable death? To an untouchable?" the chief spat contempt once again, "An untouchable can never expect honour even in death. An untouchable is footwear whose place is determined by the *shastras*. He will live in filth and die in filth, that's all."

"He is a human being rendered untouchable by your society. He is as much a child of God as you, sir. Why, then, this discrimination? God's compassion reaches out equally to all. You people hamper its rendering," Lakhan's desperate argument.

"Human being? Yes." The chief avoided Lakhan and looked at Jamuna who was listening to the arguments as a mute witness. "Your women are the only human beings amongst you, untouchables. Look at her, she is so beautiful and worthy of a man's desire. She can set you free if you so desire", said the chief while staring at Jamuna lustily.

"What do you mean?"Asked Lakhan who had suspected the man's lecherous intention, "what do you mean by that?"

The chief smiled and, looking at the men who stood surrounding him, said—"tell him the meaning."

"Lakhan", said one of the men, "It's simple. Send your wife to *haveli* tonight and tomorrow you will be free".

Jamuna stood still as if afflicted by snakebite while Lakhan started shivering with anger. He lost control over himself, stretched both his hands towards the chief who was standing close by, got hold of his throat and began to strangle him with enormous strength. The man screamed for help in choked voice and received it within no time. The four men that stood behind him came to his rescue. They pulled Lakhan away and began to beat him brutally. Lakhan tried to resist but they overcame him soon. The chief was free and now it was his turn.

He procured a heavy stick from one of his men and began to thrash Lakhan with it. The stick fell down heavily upon Lakhan's head, jaw, shoulder and back. Lakhan tried to ward him off the stick with hands and tried to reach out to the chief. But he was exhausted and his resistance came to an end. He fell down on the ground. The chief kicked him repeatedly while he lay motionless. Now the chief himself was tired. He left Lakhan lying in a pool of blood and went away. The men followed him.

Jamuna watched the scene with dazed eyes. As she realised the situation she ran towards her husband. She held her husband's head on her lap and began to cry. She pleaded for help to the onlookers whom she knew very well. No one came forward. They all went away quietly. She now began to talk to her husband who seemed to have moved a little.

"Are you alright, tell me. Are you alright?" She asked him.

"Yes I am alright. Let's go home", he said.

Lakhan tried to raise himself and sit up. But he found it difficult. Jamuna put her arm beneath his head and offered him support. She wiped away blood from his face and helped him stand up. She took his arm over her shoulder. They walked slowly towards home while men and women watched them with sympathy.

No one came to enquire about Lakhan's plight. His own people whom he had helped in time of need and who used to visit his house just to talk to his old parents did not turn up. Jamuna applied home-made medicine to the wounds and swollen places on her husband's body. He was recovering slowly but was shattered within. He kept on brooding when left alone in the house. The entire world outside had turned hostile against him. His inability to protect his wife's honour made him ashamed of himself. How can he feed his little children and old mother if the entire village refuses to offer him job? Where shall he go in time of crisis? No solution seemed to be within reach. Jamuna, who had been watching her husband's demeanor closely, made a suggestion—they will leave the village and settle down elsewhere temporarily. Migration was the only practical remedy to a problem which had shaken the very root of existence.

Lakhan was lost in a series if thoughts while Jamuna made preparations to leave. She packed things in bundles to be carried on heads. Her father-in-law was an industrious man who had built the house and bought valuable things. She will miss them all. She has witnessed the glory of the house when the entire locality—the untouchables—called on her father-in-law with respect. Many came to him for advice, others for help, still others to seek his interference in a domestic feud. She herself was treated like *lakshmi* in the house. Jamuna's eyes moistened as the past memories welled up.

For Lakhan's old mother it was a disaster. She had spent her entire life time here, collected bitter-sweet experiences, and had become one with the very soil itself. She had interacted with everyone in the village, shared joys and sorrows with every one, why no one comes forward to help her son now that he needs it? Her last wish was to lay down her body in a grave beside her husband's on the bank of the river. Where shall she breathe her last now? Why didn't she die earlier? Why did Lakhan's father leave her behind and went away?

Lakhan lifted the big bundle and put it on his head. Jamuna picked up another. She asked her mother-in-law and the children to follow her. They left the house with heavy heart and came near the shrine. Lakhan's old mother folded her hands in the direction of the Goddess and muttered something to her. Lakhan remembered the day when he refused to obey the chief's command and took his father's dead body to the graveyard through the same lane. He was also reminded of the punishment meted out to him. 'Is he *contrite* about the act? No, not at all,' he told to himself. On the contrary, he was proud of what he did. He performed the filial duty to satisfaction. He loved his father and was ready to suffer for the sake of love.

They came out of the village and halted at a place to have a last look. Lakhan turned back and saw the cluster of small houses. He could locate his house which stood apart from the huts that surrounded it. He was not certain if he could ever come back and occupy the house again. He must bid farewell to it, temporarily though. He looked ahead on the way and started walking. Jamuna followed him with her children and the old mother-in-law. They soon disappeared in the thick forest.

# 4

# When the Sun God Refused to Set

Raghoba lost his wife when he was young. He was physically capable of hard work and had good looks. Besides, he had reputation of a nice person; friendly, amiable and cooperative. His friends and relatives suggested that he should remarry. Any girl in the neighbourhood will accept him as husband and be his second wife. He, however, declined their suggestion and decided to bring up his two kids whom he loved. His wife had named their children—girl and boy—as Kala and Babu. Kala was the firstborn and three years older than Babu. She must have been five years of age when her mother died. That means Babu was two years old. Raghoba's unwillingness to remarry was the result of his love for his wife who had passed away unexpectedly, leaving him with the two little souls who needed to be brought up with love and care. Raghoba did not want to spoil the domestic atmosphere and place his children in trouble by bringing stepmother in the house.

When Raghoba went away to work Kala took over the domestic responsibilities. She would cook, clean and look after the little Babu. Babu was a motherless child and every care was taken to fill that void so that he grows up like a normal boy.

When Raghoba returned home after work his heart would throb with pride to see his children doing well. He wanted to enroll Kala in school but girls' education was not common during those days. Besides, her presence at home was valued above everything else. However, he would certainly educate his son and send him to school when he is old enough for that.

Raghoba would rise early in the morning and offer prayers to the Sun God as soon as he appeared on the horizon. It was the old habit he inherited from his father. That would give him strength for the day's work and keep his spirit genial for the rest of the day. He would pray for his children's welfare and for his own ability to raise them properly so that his wife above in the heaven can smile on her children's good fortune. Raghoba was addicted to this praying habit so much so that when there was no sun in the sky, and this would happen many a time during monsoon, he would not eat even a morsel of food on that day. However, his concern for the children would continue as usual.

Seasons changed and years passed. Raghoba's children were grown up now. Kala grew into a matured girl with a sense of duty and responsibility. Babu's education continued. He was not very intelligent as his school record showed, nevertheless, he possessed the practical sense of getting through examinations. He passed tenth standard with significantly good result. Raghoba had plans to send him to college as monthly stipend and annual scholarships were available for boys and girls from his community. Though Raghoba was a bit unwilling to send his son away, he decided against his personal weakness and enrolled the boy in a college at a town not far away from his village. Meanwhile, he had started looking for a suitable groom for his daughter whose marriage was a big responsibility for a doting father who had already set aside a sum of rupees for the expenses likely to incur.

Kala had good looks. Her homely appearance made her an easy choice for the future in-laws. Raghoba invited all his relatives and the entire neighbourhood for his daughter's marriage. It was, so to say, a grand marriage ceremony of a poor widower's only daughter. Kala went away to her in-laws leaving her father lonely and desolate. Now, he had to cook his food himself, go to day's work and spend sleepless nights alone as Babu was away studying in collage at the town. He would lie on a cot, alone in the darkness of night, and think of the days that were now no more. The images of his wife and daughter would float before his eyes till sleep finally fell slowly upon his tired eyelids.

Age has its toll on the rich and poor alike. The poor, however, resist its march stoically while the rich seek refuge in pills and pandemonium. Raghoba was past the youth now, and reached the stage when man looks around for a reliable support. Not that he suffered from some physical ailment, no. Raghoba, on the contrary, enjoyed good health. It was on certain occasions that he lapsed into emotional emptiness and felt like a destitute. These moments would drive him mad. He would search for something, he presumed, is lost, but never able to recollect its form or appearance. The momentary struggle would exhaust him and he would find himself lying on the ground and would feel as if come around after a prolonged *inebriation*. He would try to remain as composed as possible not to let such attacks reccur. But the loss of control over himself became quite frequent and the neighbours were convinced that Raghoba was sick.

Babu was quite attached to his father and knew that his father has scarified entire life to raise him properly. He remembered how his demands as a child were met promptly, Kala's came next. He also remembered the days when his father would offer his own share to little Babu and remain himself without food. He also knew well enough that Raghoba was old now and needs to be taken care of. He came home from the town one day and declared that he has relinquished education and decided to look after his father. Raghoba was surprised at his son's decision and tried to persuade him—

"Don't give up education in the middle. Continue till you obtain at least a degree. Don't bother about me too much."

"How will you manage alone? Who will take care of you in sickness?" asked Babu.

"Who told you I am sick?" Raghoba was annoyed. "I sometimes get a delusion, that's all. That's not sickness." He told his son emphatically.

"That can be dangerous, particularly, if there is no one around", Babu told him.

"So what? Are you going to waste your life looking after an old, useless man?"Raghoba's annoyance grew stronger. "Why don't you complete education and get a nice job?"

"And leave you alone to suffer?"Asked Babu.

"Try to understand, son, you have the whole life lying ahead of you. I am a ripened leaf of a tree. Can drop down any moment. There is no point in running a business unlikely to yield benefits." Raghoba tried to rationalise the situation.

Babu remained unmoved by Raghoba's argument. He knew that the man wants to continue playing the role of a sacrificing father as long as he lives. He did not go to town again, instead, began working in the village itself and settled down at home. He was not well built physically and lacked the expertise of a manual worker. Therefore, no one would hire him for field work. There was no other work available in the village, or around it. Raghoba approached the head of the village panchayat with the request to incorporate his son somewhere within the set up and give him a job that would meet the family's meager requirements. The village *panchayat* knew the man as honest and sincere person and his truncated efforts to educate his son further. Everyone was willing to help him out. Babu was qualified to manage the office affairs which included simple things like writing letters to the higher authorities at *taluka* place, maintaining records etc. He was offered an official position in village *panchayat* carrying remuneration of a sum good enough to meet the expenses.

Raghoba could find peace with himself. The daily routine of prayers to the Sun God became longer as he could afford to dedicate more time to them. He had stopped going to work as his son had bid him stay at home and rest. To rest the whole day at home doing nothing would mean to indulge in emptiness and to become an easy prey to the aberrations he experienced once. Raghoba was not aware of their precise occurring. He only had heard people talking about them and their ill-effects on his flawless personality. He could hardly understand the meaning of references they inferred. He, however, did not want to invite any blemish and decided to remain as alert and within control of himself as possibly he could.

It was long since Kala had left for her in-laws. She was a mother of a child now. She was happy to know that her brother has got a job in the village itself and that he is looking after his father very well. Whenever she visited her father's house the memories of childhood filled her heart with pleasure, now that Babu, whom she had raised with affection, was an earning hand and supporting the household with full responsibilities. She knew her father's illness, but has found him always cheerful in her presence and wondered why people say so many unpleasant things about the ailment. Finding herself alone with her father one day, she opened up a topic which was nagging Raghoba himself for quite sometimes.

"How long will you cook meals for you and your son? Why don't you bring daughter-in-law, now that Babu is old enough and earning?" she asked her father.

Raghoba was not surprised at his daughter's question. He smiled at her and asked—"Do you have any good girl in mind? Tell me if you have, and I will talk to Babu today itself."

"I don't have anyone in mind, but there can be many girls suitable for Babu's stature. We only need to search for one", said Kala.

Babu was not very keen on getting married as it was just over a year that he had started earning. He wanted to build a larger house to accommodate many people. He always felt embarrassed whenever guests arrived, particularly his sister's in-laws, because the house his father has inherited from his father, presently occupied by him, was no better than a hut—four muddy walls and the hay stack roof above covered with ordinary slates. Raghoba had extended the front portion by erecting a room like structure which was being used as kitchen. Where will he put his wife after marriage and where will his father sleep? He argued with his father. Raghoba explained to him that house was not the priority, other things came first. Presence of a woman in the house makes it a temple; she is the *Lakhmi* residing therein who not only prepares meals for men but also makes it a worthy place to live in. Besides, his father would like to see grandchildren playing around before he closed his eyes once and for all. Was it not his obligation to fulfill his father's last desire? Babu was at his wit's end and gave in to his father's persuasion.

Thus began the search for Babu's bride. A girl from a closeby village was found suitable for the purpose. A good looking girl of eighteen who professed skill and expertise in housekeeping and willingness not only to put up with the old in the family but also to take proper care of them. Her parents called her Baby and appeared perfect match for the young Babu. When Babu's marriage ceremony came off to everybody's satisfaction, Raghoba felt his another dream was fulfilled.

When Baby arrived as a newly wed girl to her husband's house she was a bit puzzled. She had not gone to college for education like her husband and thought herself inferior to the college-educated Babu. She, however, had gone to school and received formal education. She could read and write very well. Babu never thought of his wife's education and was delighted to receive a beautiful wife who would make the home happier. Raghoba wanted to rename his daughter-in-law but was convinced by his son that the name sounds perfectly matching to his own with difference only of one syllable. Satisfied by his son's explanation Raghoba thought that his son and daughter-in-law are made for each other. They are the couple of *Lakshmi-Narayan*.

Baby's parents took her to their house immediately after marriage and sent her back to her in-laws once again after a week's period. The process of marriage consummation begins now. That was a convention among the *Mahars* –the community to which Raghoba belonged. He received his daughter-in law with eagerness as she would fill the void created by his wife's sudden demise several years ago. He thought of his wife and imagined how happy she would have been, had she been alive today. She would have made all the preparations for her son's wedding night. 'Never mind', he told to himself, 'I shall do it myself'. He busied himself the whole day in decorating that part of the house where the couple would spend the night together. When Babu came back home after work in the evening he found his father waiting for him like a young mother waiting for her child returning home from school. He knew his father's doting love for his son, who, he believed, is still a kid. But the overflowing joy that was evident from Raghoba's profile was beyond the stretch of his imagination.

Meals got over around nine thirty, the usual time of dinner for the Indian villagers. Babu was left alone with his young wife by his father who quietly came out of the inner yard of the house and made his bed in the front portion which he found quite convenient for the purpose. He lied down on the cot with closed eyes and tried to sleep. Sleep, however, refused to oblige. He began to turn sides and realised that he was thirsty. He had forgotten to place a glass of water beside his bed. He stepped down and went to the door. He was about to push it open but realised that it would be a mistake. He knew that the young couple inside will not relish interference. He returned to his place and tried to make himself comfortable. There was no rest and no comfort around the corner. Raghoba, on the contrary, began to feel restless. He came out, answered the nature's call and went back to the cot. Thirst seemed to have caught him by throat and he felt dry. He must procure a glass of water and drink immediately. He went ahead and threw the door open which seemed to have been left undocked. The young couple had just begun to move ahead in the course of conjugal act when Raghoba thorough fared their privacy. He looked around as if to supervise the act. It was quite visible in the dim light of the flickering lamp. "Father", Babu exclaimed in surprise and Baby let out a scream as she tried to cover herself with the sari that lay crumpled on the ground. "Father, father", Babu's repeated calls brought Raghoba to himself. The realisation of the situation drowned him in shame and he rushed back to his place in a state of frenzy.

Next morning the sun rose late. Raghoba was impatient to offer his daily prayers to the Sun God and narrate to him the last night's incident. He wanted to do penance to atone for the sin he committed. When the sun rose finally he lay prostrated on the ground facing east till Babu came and lifted him up. He had found nothing wrong in his father's behaviour last night because to enter the inner yard of the house was his routine and a prerogative though executed at a wrong moment of time. He took him inside where Baby waited with a cup of tea. Raghoba sipped tea out of saucer averting Baby's eyes and quietly came out to rest on the cot.

Babu went away to work at the usual hour. Baby was left alone at home with her father-in-law. She had deep reverence for the old man which seemed to have shaken a little after his encroachment in her private world. She had not forgotten the discomfort she felt when he saw her naked in the arms of her husband. She had lost her desire after the event but could give in to her husband's only not to displease him. Babu had tough time to convince her of his father's ignorance and unintentional act. She seemed to have developed a grudge against the old man. Therefore, when she offered him the noon meal it was an act of mechanical servitude; no words exchanged between the two. Raghoba ate the food silently and left the place. He slept well in the afternoon while Baby waited anxiously for her husband's arrival.

Babu arrived home in the evening and went straightway inside to his wife. Raghoba, who watched his son going, was hurt. Never before his son was so indifferent as to neglect his old father standing in the way, he thought. He smiled to himself and found a place to sit down. A few minutes later, he saw Baby approaching with tea. She handed the saucer and cup to him and returned. Raghoba emptied the cup and placed it on the ground. Baby did not come to collect it. Raghoba, used to manage his own affairs, decided to take the things inside himself, but could not dare so because he knew his sudden entry will put the couple in disarray. He called out to Baby asking her to collect the cup and saucer and went away, probably to meet some acquaintance in the locality.

It was the time for dinner when Raghoba returned home. Baby served the meals and waited on the two while they ate. Beds were prepared. Raghoba did not forget to place a pot of water beside his bed with a glass accompanying it. He asked Babu to close the door with the bolt properly done. Time paced away slowly as Raghoba began to feel emptiness around. The night assailed him with piercing darkness and he, overwhelmed with fear, began to cry like a child lost in the crowd. Someone should take me by the hand, let someone ...but there was no one within sight. He stepped down the cot and began to walk towards the inner yard of the house which he found blocked by the door.

"Who is inside? Who is in...?" He called out loudly.

Babu, half-clad, opened the door. Deep annoyance reflected on his face. "What's wrong with you", he asked his father. "Why can't you sleep and let us sleep as well? Go, please go", he announced and closed the door against his father.

The following day turned out to be cloudy from the morning itself and Raghoba could not offer his prayers to the Sun God. He declined the morning tea offered by Baby and refused to eat for the day. Babu knew his father's attachment to the Sun God and hoped that the divine ball of fire will soon emerge out of the clouds allowing his father to eat. He went to work and on his return found that his father was still asleep. It was almost the evening and the darkened horizon did not reveal the setting sun.

Babu went to his father and asked him to get up. "Get up father, get up. Its evening and time for you to eat." There was no response from the old man. Babu went up to him and shook him by the shoulder, and, as he turned him to a side, realised that his father had breathed the last.

Babu was dumbfounded with grief. His father had died without eating. He looked towards the west. The Sun God appeared quite prominently on the horizon. He looked at the sun and felt that the sun shares his loss and will not set today.

# 5

# And Quiet Flowed the Purnamai...

Not very long years ago, the river Purna had enriched the villages situated on its bank. Those were the days when the villagers took pride in their association with the river whose sweet water quenched their thirst. A dive in the river would free them from the weariness of the daily routine; the sins they committed inordinately would be washed away in the flow of the river. Purna for them was as holy as the Ganga itself and they all affectionately called the river *Purnamai*- Purna, the mother.

*Purnamai* offered her water equally to all the villagers who were divided into castes and communities. There were the Brahmins, the Patels, who counted themselves among the Kshatriyas, the traders who ran small shops and grinding mills and the lower castes treated as untouchables. The Muslims also formed a sizable portion of the village population. The untouchables, however, were a caste apart. They toiled the whole day and received a tiny share in return which was never enough to feed their kinsfolk who lived huddled together in hut-like apartments. These castes served others in the village–cleaned their courtyards, reared their cattle, procured wood for cooking meals, lit the pole lamps to lighten the streets, ran with messages from village to village and, in absence of doctors and medical facilities, the untouchable women supervised their childbirths. The traditionally assigned jobs were performed with immaculate perfection, and if, by chance, anything was missed out, or gone wrong, they received abuses and humiliation. They were being oppressed by the social order for centuries together and no one, not even God whom they worshipped day in and day out, would liberate them from the dehumanising social apathy.

There were three separate *ghats* along the river flow used by three different communities. The first one, from where the water ran downward, was used by the higher castes, the Muslims used the next, and the last one was given to the untouchables. There was the fourth *ghat* allocated for cattle to drink. These spots were compartmentalised institutions and no one would trespass from one to another; not even animals would dare to drink from a spot preserved for the human beings.

Viren Patel, popularly known as Viru Bhai, ran the village administration. His forefathers ruled the vicinity during the colonial period and were in good books of the Britishers. The Patels were benevolent rulers and took proper care of their subjects. They would see that the social structure laid down by the *shastras* is maintained and everyone transacts according to the *dharma*. The survivors of the *raj* would recall how the Patels turned brutal against the offenders of *dharmashastra,* and had ordered castration of a Bramhin called Sajjan Bhat because he was caught mating with an untouchable woman in the premises of Ram temple. When the news of Bajirao Peshwa's official involvement with Mastani, the Muslim woman, reached the Patels, they immediately denounced the act. Viru Bhai, a true inheritor of the social legacy left behind by his ancestors, wanted to run the village affairs in a way that would make his forefathers proud.

Independence brought changes in the fortunes of the Patels. Most of the cultivable land was taken away by the government and given to the tillers. That being the only source of wealth, Viru Bhai's affluence deteriorated. He had a large family and a hugh mansion to look after. Polygamy among the ruling castes was a social practice when Viru Bhai was young. So he married twice and had five children, three from the first wife and two from the second. When he lost his second wife to an unknown disease he felt unarmed and married for the third time at the age of sixty five. His third wife was about twenty two years of age. He was particularly fond of this young girl, who, in return, detested her husband's unproductive advances. She found nothing fascinating about the old man whose grey hair reminded her of a grandfather who had recently died of cardiac arrest.

Viru Bhai had put his young wife in a separate room of the enormous mansion which needed repairs and renovations from every side. The mansion was the symbol of power and glory the Patels had enjoyed once. Now it appeared like *scrotum* of an old man suffering from hydrocele, trying to uphold itself from one side and in total disruption from another. Viru Bhai wanted to renovate the mansion, or at least put some of its parts in order,but he had no money and would get nothing on credit as all creditors had refused to oblige him anymore. Viru Bhai would curse this ungrateful lot who had once begged at his father's feet for everything they possess now. 'Ah', he would think with a profound sense of loss, 'if only the hands of clock could be reversed'.

Viru Bhai's young wife, whom he named Lila, was always alone at home and wanted to roam about in the open air, particularly in the afternoon, when her husband was away at work. Sushilaben, Viru Bhai's first wife, an elderly woman in her late fifties and a motherly figure to Lila, was taken aback when Lila asked her if any of her children would accompany her to the river bank for a leisurely walk in the afternoon as there were less people around at that time. The very thought of a Patel woman walking alone leisurely on the river bank was as alien to

Sushilaben as a trace of human existence on the Mars to an astronaut. She thought it a proper opportunity to talk to her husband who had always been elusive to her approaches and tried to avoid confrontations with the once ruling female spirit of the mansion. She, somehow, got hold of the man when he was trying to frisk towards Lila's room and asked him angrily—

"Have you lost all your senses and become blindfolded to the events in the mansion?"

Sushilaben's assertive voice always had devastatating effects on Viru Bhai. He had tied the conjugal knot with her some fifty years back, and married another woman immediately after they had their firstborn. He, then, spent most of his time with the second woman, visiting Sushilaben on and off. She felt humiliated but bore up her spirit knowing that the number of wives of the Patels determines their social status. She did not want the Patel clan to be counted anywhere less than other families in their community. She tried to hold her family's honor high at a time when the government stripped it off by taking away everything that made them a ruling caste. She had requested her father to come to their rescue, who had willingly donated a few acres of land to Sushilaben and her children. Her father's generous gesture helped the family survive. Viru Bhai's indomitable pride was hurt and he decided to marry for second time hoping that the marriage would fetch him a fortune. His second wife, however, brought nothing with her except promises that remained unfulfilled till her untimely death. After that, he heard nothing from his dead wife's father. He, therefore, had to live under perpetual obligation of Sushilaben who spared no occasion to remind the man of his desolation. She did not oppose her husband's third marriage because she knew that the man had already over utilised his youthful vigour and was a hollow structure likely to faint with a slight movement of the waist. Besides, the honour of the ruling clan—the Patels—relied on the number of wives a man has.

When Viru Bhai heard Sushilaben's derisive voice he did not stop. The woman almost yelled at him and asked—

"Have you also gone deaf? Did you hear what I say?"

"What is it?" Viru Bhai turned his head towards her and asked.

"Don't show off your virility like a young man of twenty. It's a matter of past now. Better pay attention to present reality and listen carefully to what I tell you," Sushilaben's voice had a tone of authority.

Viru Bhai stopped as if by command. He turned back and stood facing his wife. He looked at her inquiringly as she spoke—

"That *maharani* you brought home wants to move out and wander when you are away. Tell her to behave like a Patel woman and preserve whatever little honour is left."

Viru Bhai did not understand what she said. He, therefore, asked her blankly—

"What does that mean?"

"Go to your *pattarani* and ask it to herself", Sushilaben almost pushed him into Lila's room and turned back. Inside, Lila was making herself up to welcome her husband. She knew the old man's impotent infatuation for her and allowed him to caress her at times. Viru Bhai found her immensely desirable on these occasions though the desire itself would desert him impromptu. He, then, would tell her stories of his childhood days till the girl slipped into deep slumber.

When Viru Bhai entered Lila's room she welcomed him with bewitching smile. He sat down on the enormous bed which had been recently shifted to his young wife's room from the one where it was lying useless after the sudden demise of his second woman. Lila watched his face and realised he had some queries. She sat close to him and asked endearingly—

"What is it? Why do you look so worried?"

"Ah, yes," he said, "Did Sushila say anything to you today or maybe yesterday?"

"No no", replied Lila, "I asked her to send someone with me as I want to go out for a walk in the afternoon."

"Is it necessary?" Asked Viru Bhai who seemed to have been puzzled at his wife's unusual explanation? "Women don't go for walk, not at least from our family."

"Not even with their husbands? Why don't you come with me if you can manage?" Asked Lila with a little nervousness.

"Me? Oh no." Said Viru Bhai, thinking of the people who would laugh at his late life adventure. "I cannot," he said again, "but I will arrange to send someone to accompany you. I will ask Ajban to send his daughter who has learnt a few books and is a clever girl. She will be a nice company to you, I am sure."

Ajban was an untouchable who had served the Patels for several years. He had left the Patels as he had received land from the government and was its owner now. He worked hard and cultivated the land which yielded good harvest. He had sent his children to school and then to college. His son, Baiju, was twenty four years of age while daughter, Bijli, twenty. Ajban had other children too; presently, however, he had decided to look for a permanent settlement of these two either by getting them married, or by finding jobs for them. Baiju and Bijli were at home when Viru Bhai himself came to meet Ajban and asked for Bijli's company to his wife Lila whenever she desired to walk along the river bank. Bijli herself had agreed to the proposal as the thought of escorting the Patel's wife along the river bank thrilled her. Viru Bhai had asked her to reach the mansion every day around four o'clock in the afternoon where she could have some eatables and tea, and move around in a manner that would pacify all.

When Lila came out in the open she found herself released as if she had been in prison all these years. The two women would stand on the river bank watching the water gliding along. The trees, the blue sky above and solitary clouds, and the cattle grazing at a distance would please Lila. She would be greeted by the women who knew her though the number of such women at that odd hour was less. She, however, wanted to avoid them all and enjoy her newly acquired freedom. Bijli was amused at her childlike exposition and wondered how she could put up with the suffocating atmosphere inside the old mansion. The two got along well with each other and, in the course of time, became trusted friends. Bijli would accompany Lila back to the mansion and return home before the nightfall.

The unexpected rain disarrayed the two women's plan when they were returning from their daily walk. Bijli took the Patel's wife to her house to protect her from the pouring rain as to reach out to the mansion within time seemed impossible. Baiju was alone at home when the two arrived. He had not seen the Patel's young wife before, though he had heard about her quite often. He knew that his sister escorts her everyday along the river bank but never expected her to be his guest. He immediately offered a chair to Lila and asked his sister to prepare tea. Does she mind accepting hospitality from an untouchable? Asked Baiju when his sister went away in the kitchen.

"No no," said Lila. "I find nothing wrong in that. Are we not, Bijli and me, friends now? To have tea at a friend's house is always good."

"You are right, but people don't think so, considering the caste factor," Baiju told her.

"Why to think of caste when we can do well without it?" Lila looked at Baiju and realised that he has good looks. The curly hair adorned his face splendidly and his eyes seemed to have something to convey. What it is, Lila wondered.

The sudden silence that befell in Lila's speech excited Baiju. He was not certain about its meaning but felt relieved when he saw her smiling at him again. Why Bijli doesn't come out as yet, he thought, and, to continue the conversation, asked—

"How is Viru Bhai? Must be very busy these days."

Lila laughed at the mention of her husband. Baiju noticed some sort of sarcasm in her laughter which indicated that Viru Bhai was an unwelcome topic at this moment. She answered his question the way she desired—

"Busy he always is, but not as busy as you are. Bijli tells me that you read a lot, and help your parents whenever possible."

"No no, not really. Just a little. That's all," he said. Lila found him shy and cordial. She liked the way he talked and answered her questions. She would have dragged him into further queries, had they not been interrupted by Bijli's delayed entry. Bijli had prepared *bhujias* which tasted delightful and the tea she offered was additional pleasure.

Viru Bhai's snoring habits had already spoilt Lila's several nights earlier; tonight his presence in the room nauseated her. She wished him either dead or doomed. All her efforts to concentrate on Baiju's youthful image received setback by the old man's constant changing sides. She tried to visualise the smiling countenance of Baiju, his pleasant voice and the eyes that deeply pierced into her heart. O damn this man! she would curse her snoring husband, and try to bring forth the idol of her dreams. She passed the night in that precarious condition, and, when the day broke, she took an early bath and spent considerable time before the mirror. She scanned her own profile in the mirror perhaps for the first time till she was fully convinced of her charm. Finally, she thanked the mirror and rewarded her own image with big broad smile.

When Bijli came to escort her in the afternoon Lila suggested that they will not waste time in wandering aimlessly on the river bank. Instead, they will go to Bijli's house. She will sit with Baiju and listen to the stories from the town and the college which he had casually referred to yesterday. They sounded so interesting, she told Bijli, who, in response, nodded positively. "Will he be at home, at this hour of time?" Lila enquired.

"Yes, he doesn't go anywhere once he comes from the town."

"And who else?"

"No one. My parents go to work and younger siblings to school."

"Good," said Lila.

Lila frequented Bijli's house regularly and spent several hours with Baiju. She would send Bijli away on some pretext to be left alone with the young man. The two would talk ceaselessly on their expositions till they came to know each other well. Baiju realised that the young woman needs love and was gradually drawn towards her. Lila was already in deep love with him. She would forget everything in presence of Baiju including her marital status and the caste barrier that separated the two. The urge that had remained unfulfilled till now would push her into Baiju's arms whose kisses and caresses would send her wild with passion. She would tear his shirt open and reach down to his groins. Then the nature would follow its own course. Baiju, who had joined the woman in her erotic adventure rather unwillingly, had realised now that he loved her with equal intensity. He would be lost without her and, at the same time, would be agitated at the possible consequences of the affair. How could he face the Patel community and his own people for getting entangled with a high caste married woman? And a Patel woman, for that matter, who reigned supreme in the village till now and whose intimidating dominance pervaded the vicinity even now. How can a man of his position—an untouchable, a son of Patel's servant dare love the wife of his master? Lila, who had transcended all the proprieties of marriage, was happy now that she had snatched for herself what marriage failed to offer. And she would not let it go, come what may. Besides, she loved Baiju wholeheartedly as a man and as a perfect companion.

Nothing remains secret forever, not for long in a village like the one in our tale. When Sushilaben heard about Lila's scandalous affair with an untouchable boy the heavens fell down upon her. When Viru Bhai learnt it he felt like a eunuch whose genitals were lost. When other members of the Patel community knew it they all roared with anger and frustration. They gathered in Viru Bhai's mansion and sought explanation as to why did he allow his young wife to roam in the open like a heifer grazing in other man's land? Why did he not tie her down like a goat to be sacrificed? How will he restore the honour of the community? Viru Bhai was speechless as he had no answer to offer. Sushilaben suggested killing Lila and burying the dead body in the courtyard itself. Someone asked her to wait, for avenging the boy from the untouchables comes first. They must realise the repercussions of social transgression; they must be brutally punished. Yes, but Lilaben's role in the sinful act cannot be ignored, she is equally liable to be punished, an old member of the Patel clan argued. She is in the mansion, she is inside, bring her here, bring her at once.

There was no trace of remorse on Lila's face when she appeared before the gathering. She faced them boldly and answered each of the questions she was put to. Her confrontation with Sushilaben marked the event.

"You slut," Sushilaben yelled at her, "were you born to dishonour the Patel clan? Why did you not perish at the time of birth itself ? Why did you marry my husband and enter the mansion if there was such fire inside you; and you chose a *bhangi* to get screwed. How shameful, how base and despicable".

"Enough, enough," retorted Lila, "hold your tongue, Sushilaben. Remember I too posses one in my mouth."

"Have you left anything more to be explained, you bitch, after having blackened your face with an untouchable?" asked Sushilaben.

"Will you call your daughter by the same name if she is compelled to live with an old toothless bull and goes out fishing for men?" Lila asked patiently.

"Stop it, stop it at once," it was Viru Bhai who screamed at the top of his voice addressing Lila. "Stop it at once and get inside your room immediately. Otherwise..."

"What will you do otherwise, my dear husband?" Asked Lila mockingly.

"Otherwise I will kill you," said Viru Bhai as he stood up. Lila saw him shivering with anger and returned to her room quietly. Viru Bhai instructed his elder wife to keep strict watch on Lila and see that she doesn't move out of the room. That's not enough, someone told Viru Bhai, we got to get hold of that untouchable filth and wash it away from the sight. Got to get hold of the boy and kill him.

"Yes, yes. That's necessary. That's the only way of restoring honour of the Patel clan," there was a general consensus among the men. They dispersed from the mansion and went away seeking weapons on the way. They procured big heavy sticks, axes, and spears and began to move towards the untouchable *basti* causing a great deal of commotion. The passersby watched the group of about twenty men and youngsters charged with unspeakable sentiments. They watched the group in awe praying for the safety of the village and of their own.

Lila, who was shut inside her room, could realise the consequences. She could visualise the massacre, dead bodies lying scattered; Baiju's being one of them. She decided to protect him from the maddening crowd. She pretended to be ill and screamed as if in agony. Someone opened the door and Lila, brushing the person aside, made her way out. She came out of the mansion and took the shortest way she knew to Baiju's house. When she reached there the family was in deep panic. Ajban had already heard about the oncoming catastrophe and was pleading his son to leave the house and seek shelter elsewhere.

"Which place is safer? Where do you want me to go?" He asked his father.

"Go anywhere and leave us in peace, please go," Ajban yelled at his son.

A knock at the door frightened them but Lila's voice offered the relief. When Baiju open the door Lila held him by hand.

"Come, let's get away from here," she said. "Let's go. They are coming to kill you."

Encouraged and heartened by Lila's support, Baiju came out of the house. The two went to the backside and began to run like hunted deer. The only place Lila knew closely and with which Baiju was equally well acquainted was the river bank. They could locate some corner among the cliffs and lay hidden embracing each other. Lila gathered Baiju into her arms and, like a loving mother, watched his profile while he, unshackled by her adulation, felt free and liberated.

The violent mob that had reached Ajban's house was disappointed to miss the boy. They forced Ajban to reveal his son's whereabouts and the man, fearing for his life, told them that it was Lila who had taken him away he does not know where. The mention of Lila's name, at this juncture, seemed incredible, but they believed, considering her equally incredible exploits into the clandestine realm of love and sex. Get back at them, find them out, someone suggested and they all turned back in different directions. They kept inquiring the villagers and got the clue that the two lay hidden somewhere behind the cliffs on the river bank. They all rushed in that direction.

Lila and Baiju knew their fate but decided not to give in. Baiju suggested that they should swim across the river and reach out to a place from where he might collect support. They might even approach the police. There are laws in the country to protect the adult lovers. And the caste is no barrier. They heard the commotion and realised that the furious mob is close. They got up and began to move towards the river. Baiju almost dragged Lila who found it difficult to cope up with Baiju's swift movements. They reached the river bank which held before it a long stretch of deep water. If they could manage to swim across the river, the mob will not follow them and they will probably secure a safer position. For Lila it was an alien thought for she did not know swimming and the sight of deep water appealed her only from a distance. Baiju, however, was a good swimmer and was confident of carrying her across the deep water. The mob's howling came nearer and the two readied themselves to jump down the cliffs. There they are, they heard the words and flung themselves into the river. Baiju moved ahead with powerful strokes in the water and turned back to receive Lila who was trying to keep herself afloat. The clothes and the ornaments she wore pulled her down rendering Baiju's efforts to sail her through water ineffective. The violent mob reached the river bank and could locate the two lovers struggling for life. The crowd hurled abuses and pelted big sharp stones at them. It was a group of insensitive brutal men who took delight in casting afflictions on the young helpless lovers.

A stone had struck Baiju on the forehead. He was bleeding. He pulled Lila on to his back and tried to push forward in the water. It was not easy to swim across the current, quiet though it was. Stones showered on them causing injuries to heads. A huge stone fell down upon Lila's head which loosened her grip on Baiju's shoulders. She was left behind as Baiju stroked himself ahead. "Baiju, Baiju", she called him back and began to sink in the water. Baiju returned to her and tried to hold her by hand. But the flowing current had taken her away from him and she disappeared in the depth of water. Baiju located his beloved and lifted her motionless body upon his shoulders. Something heavy hit his head. It was an iron rod shot like an arrow from the crowd. It diffused Baiju's struggling spirit and he felt like a lifeless object caught in the whirlwind. He held Lila's hand firmly but the rest of her body was under water. His efforts to lift her up failed as he was totally exhausted and lay quietly on the surface of the water. Lila was breathless, smothered by the current. The two bodies, now at the mercy of the *Purnamai*, were carried away by the quiet flow of the river.

# 6

# A Tale Told by a Scavenger

My name is Sukha—Sukha Billu Bhangi-as they have written it down in the book which contains the list of many of my type—meaning, men and women engaged in the work of cleaning and sweeping the streets. My father cleaned the toilets in the government *dafter*. He left his job to me after his death as a legacy. I count myself fortunate to receive this job without efforts when hundreds of educated men and women are either unemployed or have taken jobs below their dignity. I have no dignity as it never came in my way when I went to work, or received the wages. They treated me with equal disregards and humiliation. My father had deep regards for Bapu who had promised total freedom from the serfdom. Both of them are dead now and I am left with no choice but to wait for that auspicious day. The nation has become free, they say, but what freedom means I have no inkling. My days and nights are the same as they were when my father lived. Our locality has not yet found a central place in the town and we still continue to live at the outskirts. Things have also changed, I know. Don't call me a senile old man incapable of appreciation, I am not. I know that manual cleaning of toilets are replaced by flush and our boys and girls have started going to schools as we never did before. But wait, my dear listeners, I got many startling tales to narrate tales that would require your unbiased judgment on our position in free India. Will you be so kind as to lend your ears to this tale of a poor scavenger?

...Monsoon had just withdrawn and the muddy roads were yet to take proper shape. The heat before *Dassera* had taken toll of the people who worked the whole day long. The evening had stretched its weary limbs towards darkness and I, tired after the day's work, had taken way to home. A commotion ahead caught my attention as I walked leisurely on the road. I heard a woman screaming while several men beat her up. That was a scene regularly enacted recently wherein an allegedly mad woman was penalised for her antics that caused unusual tension. She was a woman in late thirties, abandoned by her husband, who, in a state of frenzy, would abuse all her in-laws including the man who had brought her here as his legally wedded woman. She would call them nasty names and evoke curse to the entire caste. They were the Brahmins and an influential family in the town. The cause of her insanity was never known but the *infamy* she brought upon them had unsettled them socially. She had attempted to set the house on fire and attacked her husband physically, who, in return, whipped her brutally. She, then, would run out of the house, cursing and screaming, unmindful of her position, of her disposition as well. All the efforts to take her back home would be rendered futile and the event would turn out violent, as I saw it presently.

I walked past the event neglecting it but halted after a few steps as someone called me by name. I returned to the spot and saw the woman lying motionless. She had excreted copiously and was stinking of the human waste. Those who inflicted pain upon her had gone away leaving her in dirt and desolation. They had obviously called me to clean the spot without touching the woman perhaps, and, if possible, make her aware of the conditions. I did my job, sweeping the waste aside and cleaning the ground with water. The woman needed cleaning as well, so

I poured a bucket of water on her. The touch of cold water brought her back to her senses. She groaned with pain as she tried to sit up. I noticed a profound sense of pity in her eyes as she looked at me as if to demand her liberation. How can a slave liberate another of his kind, I told myself and started walking away. *No, don't leave me alone, take me away with you*, I imagined her calling me, or did she really call? I did not know. But I found myself with her again, this time, helping her to get up and walk properly. She placed her head upon my shoulder as she walked with me as if she knew me since ages to pose her trust entirely on me.

It was dark when we reached home. My parents were taken aback when they saw the woman with me. They could recognise her in the dim light of the lamp, for they had seen her many a time in the streets abusing others, or being abused by them. She was known as mad woman in the town. My father's curiosity compelled him to ask–

"Who is the woman?"

"The woman in the street. You must have seen her before". I told him.

"Why did you bring her home?"He asked again.

"I don't know." My answer.

"Where are you going to put her up?"His next question.

"I don't know". I reiterated and knew that our tiny apartment had no space to accommodate a stranger. But then, how could I leave her out in the dark at the mercy of the elements. An unknown bond was established between us two within that short span of time. Unknown fear also haunted me simultaneously. Nevertheless, I decided to allow her to stay and spend night with us.

Next day, my parents went away to work early in the morning while I stayed back. The woman did not rise till late when the noise of playing children outside woke her up. I offered her water to clean the mouth and placed a cup of tea before her. She looked fresh and not a trace of madness stained her sober face. Let me admit, dear audience, she appeared beautiful to me and wondered why did her kinsfolk treat her the way they did. She had not uttered a single word to me so far; I myself lacked courage to speak to her, knowing her superior social status. There was a strange shyness in her profile, and all our interactions till now were done with her eyes lowered down. The desire to speak to her did not remain suppressed any longer and I dared a dialogue with her.

"How do you feel now?" I asked.

"Better," she told me quietly.

"Why did those people, I mean, your in-laws and all, ill-treat you?"My next question.

"I don't know," she said.

"People say you are mad. Are you really mad?" I asked her.

"What do you think? Do you think I am mad?" She asked me looking straightway into my eyes.

I turned my face away as I had no answer to offer. I found all her demeanors sane and satisfactory. Not a sign of dementia appeared anywhere in her behaviour. Yet the whole town knew her as a mad woman. The conclusions I draw, whatever they would be, are premature, I thought and deviated the talk to another direction—

"What is your name?" I asked her trying to guess her inner thoughts.

"Mukta," she told me quietly.

The name sounded to me like any other name of an ordinary woman confined to the margins of orthodox Indian family who was obliged to beget children to her man and display enormous endurance to the afflictions caused by customary social habits. I could bleakly surmise the cause of Mukta's plight—that she must have, at some point in the course of time, refused to conform to the norms. That, however, was a vague guess and I dismissed it with a stroke of *indifference*.

Contrary to my expectations and fear, nobody came in search of Mukta. She, however, had become an object of amusement for the people in our locality. Children gathered to see her and the grown-up considered her presence as unusual. She had put on clothes that did not really set her apart from our own women, but her personality gave out an enigma of an outsider. She was good-looking with striking features though mutilated by the circumstances, and her mannerisms revealed her refined inner being. Although pronounced as mad by the society, there was method in her madness.

My own position, however, was precarious. I feared an onslaught by Mukta's men who would think it deplorable to see their woman, abandoned though she was, at a scavenger's house, and scheme out some plan to persecute me. It was difficult for me to convince myself and be reconciled to the situation while Mukta dwelt in a fancied castle-invulnerable, invincible and imperishable by the ways of the world. I had brought her home, but the home itself seemed to be on the brink of ruin when my parents threatened to quit unless I take the woman back to the place from where I had picked her up. They told me that poor though they are, have no habit of eating the leftover, that they do not pick up rags thrown out in the streets. My mother was particularly severe with the issue. She derided me for my alleged intention to beat the worn out drum. In fact, I had no intention to retain Mukta and was keen on seeing her off, yet the inward voice warned me against leaving her alone to be mocked at and abused by the street walkers. The possibility of her husband taking her home was ruled out, for, no one had bothered to inquire her whereabouts till now, neither a word of message was received though men and women had watched us walk together towards the scavenger *basti*. I served the afternoon meal to Mukta which she ate quietly, and, as the day passed on gradually, a sense of settled calmness perched on me.

The evening was tumultuous. My parents had returned home after the day's work. They flared up to see Mukta comfortably seated inside the house. They considered her as an intruder whose presence pinched them like a thorn in the flesh. Above all, they considered her as a calamity—a mad woman who can turn against her saviour in the time of crisis; a high caste arrogance that considers compassionate labour as legal servitude. My father pleaded me not to fish in troubled water as there are no gains likely to incur out of hopeless situation. My mother warned me against the possible consequences of keeping a Brahmin woman out of her senses who has already caused a considerable dishonour to her own caste and community. Will it not be imprudent of me, she asked, to pity a woman who doesn't deserve it? I could realise my parents' anxiety fully well, also their sense of social insecurity in the face of unexpected communal barbarism. I, however, thought it as a remote possibility unlikely to occur in near future. The thought of Mukta, bereft of hope and reason, impelled me to my own conclusions. I set aside all the objections raised by my parents and decided to have my own way. I told them that to leave Mukta in the present conditions would be cowardice and to desert her an inhuman act. My father retaliated relentlessly that there is no place for the two of us in his house and that I shall have to make my arrangements elsewhere if I want to keep the woman. He commanded me further to take Mukta out of his house immediately. We had to leave.

We spent the night out in a corner of the temple which I used to clean daily in the morning. The night was warm as the cold had not yet set in, but the late hours made us shiver slightly. Mukta drew close, as if by instinct, and held me in her arms. I could feel her heaving breasts pressed against my chest and her warm breath warding me off from the settling cold. We lay quietly in that position for sometimes. The ringing bells of the temple woke us up. It was the day break and the early worshippers had gathered to offer the morning prayers. They watched us with amusement–the mad woman and a scavenger sleeping in each other's arms as if wedded to fate which would lead them to doom. We parted hurriedly and tried to make ourselves comfortable to face the people gazing at us. Mukta's behaviour during these puzzling moments was entirely normal as if she had never been *demented*. It was me, on the contrary, who seemed to have lost senses at times. I was angry with myself, because my anger against the people, or against anybody else for that matter, including my parents, would have been impotent. How could I get angry with others while I myself indulged in an act which did not have social sanction? I was angry with myself also because I had not planned our elopement properly and had become an object of ridicule in the eyes of people. It was Mukta who initiated the move out of the temple and led me away into the dusk while I, diffident in my motive, followed her like a child. There was no place which could offer us shelter, there was no human being who could extend sympathies to us, and not even God seemed to be compassionate towards our plight. We reached the bus depot from where outstation buses plied. I had used the station quite sometimes earlier and knew the operations therein. We refreshed ourselves using public lavatories and bought something to eat with the money which, fortunately, was left in my pocket. Our mission was now to find a safer place which could accommodate us and offer us courage and strength. I was reminded of a distant relative living at the other end of the town. The woman, who had lost her husband long back, and had no children, lived alone. She appeared to me like a lighthouse to a ship that has lost its directions. She, in fact, had invited me several times before; my own indifference towards her was the cause of distance. I decided to seek refuge under the old woman's tutelage and renew the fading acquaintance.

The woman was delighted to see me and received us with stretched arms. She had mistaken Mukta for my wife and opened up the room in her house that was vacant and unused. I had concealed Mukta's identity from her, in view of the fact that she, like my parents, would not approve of our relationship—relationship, which did not exist at all. I had to exploit her innocence and gullibility to makes us comfortable, temporarily though. I told all the lies about Mukta that could possibly convince the woman of her authentic character. Fully convinced, she gazed at Mukta's face, which she found quite agreeable, and blessed her wholeheartedly. She arranged everything for us two—Mukta and me—under the unshakable belief that we were a legally married couple. She offered meals and clothes, and made bed for us at night.

Mukta's role in the story, dear listeners, was rather dubious. She had enacted a mute doll all through these hours showing her consent to all that I had made up. As I reflected on the day's events lying beside her that night, the flickering lamp went off. As if waiting for the moment, she turned the side and pushed herself close to me. The natural urges that cannot show off in the glaring daylight of the sun wake up in dark, and operate through the human limbs. The touch of Mukta's body enlivened the desire that lay dormant in me. I held her close and groped for her blouse. She responded likewise baring my chest and caressing it. We then reached out to each other's lower garments and removed them. I never had a woman before and the one I had in my arms now was no less than a precious gem whose value I only had heard but never knew. She had given herself totally in to me, and, like a skilled connoisseur, had taken out everything precious in me. That was the night which kept on haunting me through the rest of my life and, perhaps, changed the course of events the following day.

It was quite a pleasant morning pervading the locality of the poor. The tender rays of the sun had besmeared the muddy walls making the entire atmosphere appear bright. Women had engaged themselves in the household activities while children took delight in chasing cocks and hens around. Our host was ready with morning amenities for her guests. She offered bathing water for us and prepared breakfast consisting of sprouted cereals which seemed Mukta's favourite dish. She relished it and ate with delight and satisfaction. I had my breakfast as well and was engaged in a goodwill talk with my host whose hospitality overwhelmed my sense of gratitude. Suddenly, the host, my old aunt, pointed outside indicating something unusual. As I looked out I saw Mukta walking away in a manner as if she was a stranger heading for an unknown destination. While I called her and prepared myself to reach out to her, she disappeared from the sight. I came out and began to trace her in the street but she was nowhere to be seen. "Mukta... Mukta", I screamed out in frustration hoping for a response from a woman who has been the object of my entire attention, all my sentiments and the goal of my life. Where is she? I wondered. Has the earth engulfed her like Sita in *Ramayana*? Or has she been evapourated like the Gin in *Arabian Nights*? I went ahead in the street calling out her name, making enquiries on and off, describing her appearance to the passersby, and, telling myself not to lose hope. I was in a position of an idiot who, unable to trust his rational self, throws his sentiments away to the wind.

I had come far ahead in the town and presently found myself at the place where I had come across Mukta, two days ago, as the mad woman. I did not have precise notion of her residence but could guess the locality, now that I knew she was a Brahmin woman. I moved towards my guesswork, the posh territory of the town affluent and began to call out her name loudly. Several windows opened up at the mention of Mukta. The name seemed familiar to many as I could locate curiosity oozing out of every face that peeped through the windows. I looked around to see if Mukta responds, but my looks came back to me unresponded and the intimidating silence did not speak to me. I stood still in the midst of the road as I heard the noise from my back. "Here is the swine that defiled the sanctity of Brahmanism, the scavenger who polluted the woman of our caste". A group of about seven able-bodied men with heavy sticks in their hands came running towards me. They grabbed me by throat and began to shower punches on my body. "Get him down", someone shouted and felled me like a tree on the ground. Now they began to beat me with sticks. I screamed for help which did not come from anywhere around. So they could have their own way and continued thrashing me till they fatigued, or perhaps till I lost my consciousness.

It was afternoon when I regained consciousness. I found myself lying in excreta, in the feces and urine. I seemed to have defecated out of panic and helplessness. That must have been a way of defending me, driving enemies away like a skunk that ejects unpleasant smell when attacked. Whatever, I was at least safe, though with a couple of broken bones, presently lying in dirt. I raised myself with efforts and stood up. I did not go to my old aunt, rather chose to take the way back home...

This is the story, dear listeners, narrated not to entertain you simply, but as a slice of Indian social reality...What did you say? Sounds imaginary? Let me explain further...This is an ugly facet kept hidden from you intentionally, don't ask by whom. The *glories* of Indian narratives are too well known to be exposed further. I leave it up to you to judge and conclude. *Namaste*.

# 7

# Cobbler, Cobbler Mend My Shoe

*Cobbler, Cobbler Mend My Shoe*
*Get it done by half past two*
*If half past two is much too late*
*Get it done by half past eight...*

Sadashiv Kalel listened to his grandson reciting from the book of nursery rhymes. The child had recently been enrolled in pre-primary English medium school popularly known as kindergarten, or simply K.G. He was a retired school teacher who had come to stay with his son after he lost his wife a couple of years back. His son—Suresh—was a Government officer at district headquarters living in a recently constructed bungalow on a spacious plot of land. His wife, a graduate in Commerce, also worked in a bank. They had two children, girl and boy. Both of them went to school and, when their parents were away on duty, were left to the care of grandfather—Sadashiv Bhadaji Kalel.

Sadashiv had been a good teacher. Specialised in English and Mathematics, he knew his subjects well and took delight in his profession. After having passed matriculation he had obtained professional degree in teaching. His aspiration for college education and higher job, however, remained unfulfilled, owing mainly to poverty at home and lack of educational background. They were the cobblers, a caste in Indian social structure, who were traditionally assigned the job of shoe making. The cobblers are untouchables and form a part of the four *varnas*, the *shudras*, along with other depressed castes. Wretchedness and humiliation, combined with other degrading features, were parts of their living. They dealt in animal hide, leather and tanning the skin and finally, making shoes and other footwear. They were also required to mend them, if damaged, and make them suitable again for the wearer. Their profession was looked down upon as filthy, though it demanded a great deal of skill and dexterity, and the cobblers, ultimately, as untouchables.

*Cobbler, cobbler mend my shoe; Get it done by half past two...* Sadashiv's grandson was learning the lines by heart calling them out repeatedly. The sounding recitation led Sadashiv back into the stream of time. He remembered the days when he, as a child, helped his father mending shoes in a corner of the street to feed his hungry children...

They were always hungry, Sadashiv and his two sisters, for there was little food left after the day's meal. His mother would take care of the two little girls at home, while Sada, as he was endearingly called by his parents, was supposed to go to school. He, however, was always found sitting by his father learning the art of stitching shoes, handling mallet and leather-scraper. That was the God-given profession of the *Chamars*, his father would tell him, No *Chamar* would go hungry if he knows his profession well, while others—the *Mahars* and the *Matangs* will starve, or beg for food for lack of specific profession in the face of drought or famine. Therefore, each one of them should learn it. Sada would listen to him carefully, not to learn the profession and emulate his father, but to offer him assistance to dispose of the heap of shoes and *chappals* each one of which was labeled as urgent. Sada's father would not dare displease his customers, for they all were known faces in the village, most of them from the higher castes who would call him by his distorted first name and command him to complete the work in time. He would work hard till his fingers go stiff and face *clammy* with sweat. He worked the whole day just for a *pittance*. The remuneration for the work was meager, a coin or two, or at times, mere thanksgiving. He always returned home guilt-stricken and apologised to his wife for not earning enough...

Sada had developed liking for books and wanted to attend school regularly, but his heart would always linger around his father's tiny shop in the corner. He would run back to it during the recess and at end of the day. His father would ask him not to, rather go home and study. He would argue with his father on these occasions trying to convince him of his presence—

"How will you do all this work alone and please the customers?" He would ask.

"You need not worry about it," his father would answer, "I know my customers well and they know me very well."

"Yes, but how is it going to help you in your work? They always seem to be in hurry. Each one of them". Sada's further argument.

"They are busy people, boy, and big ones, for that matter. It's our duty to serve them with as much docility as possible". Sada's father would tell him.

"And not to receive anything in return." Sada's mocking annexure.

"That's not true. God gives us whatever is in our providence. Our job is only to work and not to expect rewards." Sada's father would tell him further.

Little Sada would find no words to argue further with his father. He, nevertheless, knew that something is missing in his father's argument. How can a man labouring the whole day around expect nothing in return? He wondered.

*Cobbler, Cobbler Mend My Shoe...Get it done by half past two...*Sada's father had just opened his shop when a customer arrived hurriedly. He left his footwear in the shop and went away with instructions to keep it ready by the time he returns. The impending work of the previous day needed attention first. So, Sada's father took it out and busied himself with it. The work took a little longer than expected and the work assigned to him by the morning customer remained unattended to. When the customer returned and noticed his footwear lying untouched he fumed with anger. "Have I not told you to keep it ready by the time I come back?"He asked.

"Yes, but other work needed priority," Sada's father answered politely. "Spare a few minutes, and I will get your work done immediately."

"How dare you keep me waiting, you pig. Do I have to spend the whole day here and leave out my other work?" The man asked excitedly.

"No no. It won't take much time. Just a few minutes." Sada's father pleaded with him.

The man, however, was in no mood to listen and reconcile to the situation. He held Sada's father by collar and pulled him. He took off his shoe and started beating with it. Sada's father offered no resistance. The man, counting shoe-beating as enough punishment, left Sada's father and went away. He, however, did not forget to threaten for further delay...

There was a marriage in the village. A girl from the rich Deshmukh family was to be wedded to a boy of equal social and economic status. Marriages in Indian villages, during those days, took place in the evening, on *goraj muhurt* in the summer season of *March and April*. That was a custom and convenience, too. The *pandal* could be erected in the open and, when the marriage ceremony got over, the guests could eat and rest in the open air of the summer night.

The entire village was invited to attend the ceremony and to eat after the guests finished their meals. The Deshmukh family received the bridegroom with customary rituals and led the *barat* with high sounding brass band. Crackers were set off and exploded. The fireworks produced noises that filled the space above. The entire village got involved forgetting the caste barriers and each individual tried to outdo another to win attention of the wealthy Deshmukhs.

The *Bhat ji* recited the last *shloka* that united the two strangers to lead the life ahead together. Flowers and grains were hurled across them as signs of blessings and the *shehnai* player began to play his instrument loudly. The ceremony, thus, came to the end with pomp and show suitable to the wedding in a rich feudal Indian family.

Sada's father waited with his wife and children outside while the rituals were performed. They were all hungry and wished the rituals get over once and for all. Several others were in similar condition, particularly those among the untouchables for whom these marriages were festive occasions when they filled their hungry stomachs with leftover of the affluent. Sada's father had instructed his wife not to cook as they were to feast at the Deshmukh *wada*. The woman felt relieved of the drudgery of the daily domestic work and blessed the Deshmukh clan profusely. They arrived rather early and waited anxiously for the moment when they will have their full meal. They had not eaten anything since morning, therefore, could hardly suppress the instinct while a variety of eatables was being served to others at a distance. The children grew restless and one of them demanded *jalebi* which she had noticed being gulped down by a guest. “Wait for sometimes,” Sada’s mother told the girl, “let the guests finish their meals first, we will have it later.”

“No. I want it now,” the girl reiterated her demand.

“Are you not a wise girl? My beloved daughter, let’s wait for some more time.” Sada’s mother tried to cajole the girl.

“No, no. I want it now, I want it now,” said the girl and began to cry. Her mother tried to hush her up but to no avail. The child raised its voice to the extent of distracting the gulping guests. The woman, exasperated by the child’s ill-timed alarm, began to thrash, causing the child scream even more loudly. Almost a scene was created out of hunger’s *irascible throes*. Men that managed the eating arrangements rushed to it and drove away the nuisance. Sada’s father pleaded for mercy and tried to explain the child’s predicament. The men were in no mood to listen to a beggar’s plea and threatened of dire consequences if persisted further.

Everything went off well as planned by the Deshmukh family, everything except one. Next morning when the bride was about to leave her parents’ house and go ahead with the groom she found her *chappal’s* belt come off. She won’t wear any other pair as this one represented the marriage sanctity and matched the garments she had put on. Men were sent for Sada’s father who was the only shoe mender available at that time. The man did his job well, stitched the belt properly, and held the girl’s foot in hand placing it inside the footwear to check its propriety. *Cobbler, Cobbler Mend My Shoe...*

Sada’s education progressed well despite the occasional hindrances. There was a general movement for education among the marginalised. Government offered scholarships to the promising boys and girls. They could afford to stay off the work and spend time in school. Sada did spend most of his time in school, but he could never forget the image of his docile father while away from him. He feared that his father would be overburdened with work and exhaust all his energy over the heap of footwear that fetch him no reward. He had heard of the shoe industry producing wealth out of the same work his father pursues. Can his father also be a millionaire some day since he knows his business so well and is capable of putting out his heart into it? He wondered. Or, why don't those industrialists—the Batas—he could recall the name, hire his father's services which could render excellent results for them? Or, can he be an industrialist himself, produce a variety of footwear and amass wealth to be utilised for the welfare of his community. How poor my people are and how helpless, he would think and would be dejected at the thought of his personal inability to do anything for them. He had heard of the movement of the untouchables led by Ambedkar, but his own people were lured away by the Congress and were overawed by Gandhi's charisma. Nevertheless, he would himself do whatever little was possible within the range of his personal capacity. He thought of cobbler's profession as noble, for it was like serving humanity in general, helping men and women in their critical moments. Therefore, he would ask his people not to forego the profession, rather pursue it with traditional zeal and comingle it with a sense of dignity. The gentry, however, would never treat the cobblers as a civilised class and looked down upon their profession as filthy. Like the rest of the untouchables in the village, they were also counted among the unholy castes.

Winter in the Indian villages is a deadly season. Like Keats' autumn Indian winter is also a season of mist and mellow fruitfulness, who fills all fruits with ripeness to the core, swells the gourd and plumps the hazel shells with sweet kernel. The season also sets budding more, and still more, later flowers for the bees, until they think warm days will never cease. While nature runs at its prime youth, winter in the Indian villages ceases the warm days for the poor and pierces the lacerating cold into their skinny limbs. There is no food enough to keep their bodies warm and no clothes to ward them off from the wintry waves. The sick and the old breathe their last and the young try to hold on to the shaky columns of life. Sada's father succumbed to the December cold. His dead body was found lying within the tiny space of the corner shop by a customer who had come to collect shoes. A mountain of calamity had fallen on Sada's family as the untimely death of his father had snatched away the source of livelihood. Sada's mother had decided to run the shop herself and continue her son's education as desired by his father. Sada tried to dissuade his mother from doing so, instead, had offered his services to look after the family. His mother, however, would not give in and sent her son to regular school while she worked herself to bring up her children. Her knowledge of the cobbler's devices was consummate and could handle the anvil, the scrapper and the stitching material with ease and perfection. Sada never wanted his mother to sit in the shop and work, for he had witnessed customers watching her swiftly moving limbs and cracking bawdy jokes. She, however, sent him away and concentrated on the work. She bore the humiliating experiences mutely while her son prepared for his examinations...

*Cobbler, Cobbler Mend My Shoe. Get it done by half past two* ... Sadashiv Bhadaji Kalel, the grandfather of the child reciting his poem, was overwhelmed with the memories of the past. The warm touch of tears running down his cheeks brought him back to the present. He looked around and noticed his grandchild smiling at him. He smiled back at the child and wondered if the little one shared his sentiments. 'No, why should he', the old man told himself, those days were marked for me alone. My progeny shall live happily ever after. The creator of the universe has rectified his mistake. No one shall command his fellow being now, no one shall compose such filthy verse and no one shall recite—*Cobbler, Cobbler Mend My Shoe...*

# 8

# Loneliness of An Ex-soldier

When Wasudeo Bhivsan Khandare opted for retirement from Indian army after serving it for fifteen years, the entire platoon thought he should continue. Wasu, as he was known among his colleagues and friends, was known for his unparalleled courage and heroism. He was placed in the Mahar Battalion after recruitment and became an integral part of it. He had shown unprecedented valour in both the wars that the nation had faced. He himself had led his unit against the hostile attack and driven the enemy away. He had carried his wounded lieutenants on back amid the shower of bullets and steered them out of danger. He faced the war time realities dauntlessly and, in the time of peace, behaved like a gentleman. Therefore, when he chose to go home permanently the regiment grew sentimental. He was given a heart rendering farewell by his seniors and fellow soldiers.

Wasu had reason to return home. He had served the nation for fifteen long years, now he wanted to serve his old parents and the community, also to do something for the village, if possible. He was a native of a small village in the western region, a remote place where modern amenities were yet to reach. He had joined army partially out of need and, partially out of patriotic romanticism. He had learnt glory of the Indian past in school. The sacrifices made by the martyrs for Independence appealed to his young sentiments, and he had decided to do something similar for the free nation. Besides, the soldier's job would fetch him regular income and facilities which the whole of his ancestry could never even dream of. He was young and well built and a few months' preparation enabled him to enroll in army as an infantry soldier.

Wasu returned home after fifteen years. Though there is a provision of annual leave for soldiers who wish to visit their kinsfolk, Wasu's involvement in the regiment affairs spared him no time and he remained away from home for fifteen long years. Much had changed since then. He was twenty when he had left home, on return, he had turned thirty five. His parents were old now and his school going sister young and beautiful. The thought of marriage had touched his mind at times but he never indulged in it for long. He had witnessed his fellow soldiers longing for their wives and sweethearts and taken pity on their conditions. He had also seen them shying away from duty when they were lovelorn or homesick. He, therefore, had decided not to marry, not at least as long as he was a duty bound soldier. His parents, who had endured a long wait and return of their son, were overjoyed to see him again. His sister's delight knew no bound. Wasu himself was delighted to be among his kinsfolk. He had bought suitable gifts for everyone, and a good amount of money he received after retirement. The government had also awarded him five acres of farming land, a fertile piece, though at a considerable distance from the village. His achievements, if at all they were to be called so, were not fortuitous, but an award of his multifarious activities and contentment. He appeared quite settled and self-assured within a short span of time after his arrival back home.

Wasu's parents wanted their son to get married and watch a grandchild toddling in the courtyard. They also wished for a descendent to carry forward their family name. "What's so great about our family?" Wasu had asked them, "And why do you need a grandson to carry it forward? Am I not alone capable of permeating all that is virtuous in your persons?"

"Yes", his parents had agreed, "but you will need yourself someone to guide you when you are old and devoid of strength."

Wasu had laughed away that thought with indifference. He could understand the relevance in his parents' argument but failed to realise its urgency. Several other things lay waiting for my attention; he told himself, my own existence comes next. The first thing to accomplish was his sister's marriage. There cannot be dearth of suitable boys, he would think, nevertheless, I will select the best one for Sumi, my darling sister.

Sumi was the short for Suman, Wasu's sister, and the one used by all to address her for all purposes. Sumi was in her prime youth now, well wrought by her creator, like a *Grecian urn*, and known for her well behaved politeness. She had looked after her parents appropriately during her brother's absence and earned the reputation of a loveable girl, capable of loving. Everybody in the neighbourhood liked Sumi for her good looks as well as for her nice, pleasant, kind and friendly behaviour. Her parents were proud of her, so was her brother. Wasu would tease her for her proposed departure to the in-law's house. She, in return, would ask him to bring her sister-in-law before she departs. The old parents would be blissfully happy to feel love operating between their off-springs.

Sumi had attended school up to tenth standard which was an agreeable norm for a village girl's education during those days. Her parents had decided not to send her to college because Wasu's retirement was due and he was to decide the future course of action. Wasu thought over the issue of his sister's further education and concluded that marrying her off was a better choice.

She can resume her education after marriage if her husband allows. They started looking for a suitable boy.

Wasu always wanted to do something for his community. They were the *Mahars,* the untouchables in the state of Maharastra, who had rendered commendable service to the society in the past and to their feudal lords within that constricted social order. They were well known for loyalty to their masters, valour and a sense of total commitment. Wasu had inherited these characteristics as a person and developed them further during the military days. The military training had also inculcated in him a civic sense and a strong will to serve humanity. He picked up his own community as an immediate object. Untouchability had rendered the *Mahars* as sub-humans. Poverty, ignorance and lack of wider social interaction had made them insensitive beasts, incapable of self-amelioration. Dr. Ambedkar's indefatigable efforts to raise them up had paid the dividends. A general awareness about human dignity and social status had spread among the *Mahars*. They had started enrolling their children in school and learnt lessons in cleanliness. They now were in a position to assert them and their identity causing heartburn to others who had looked down upon them as slaves. A new phase of revolution had set in the lives of the erstwhile untouchables. Villages across the state were brimming with enthusiasm and a new identity led them towards a wider horizon.

Revival of the Mahar battalion in the Indian army, which was due largely to the efforts of Ambedkar, had produced scope for individual skill and bravery. Several *Mahar* youths had created niche for themselves in warfare and had won coveted awards for courageous deeds. Wasu himself was honoured with the President's medal for what had been described as the "soldier's pride". Now that he was free from obligatory duties and responsibilities he could afford to spend time with the *Mahar* youths and interact with them on issues like education, sports, politics, social upliftment etc. He had become quite popular among the boys who appreciated his advice. He had gained admiration from the elders who thanked him for leading their sons on the right tracks who, otherwise were labeled as loafers.

The general atmosphere in the village, however, grew suspicious. The village authorities began to smell something foul as Wasu's radical thoughts had brought changes in their daily routine. The *Mahars* refused to offer them customary *johar* as they had been doing for generations together. They did not come begging for food on festive days. Their children attended school regularly instead of wandering in the streets, or chasing each other in the heat of the sun. This glaring change in *Mahar* community disturbed the social structure. The rich landlords fell short of labouring men who worked on their fields and cultivated their farms. They had to hire labourers from the neighbouring villages at higher remunerations. This had never happened before; therefore, Wasu's return to the village was termed as calamity. The two communities in the village—the upper castes and the *Mahars*—began to look askance on each other. A year passed in these uncertainties.

Wasu could not locate a boy of his choice for his sister because he spent most of his times on other issues. Sumi, however, was as carefree as ever. She prepared meals for the four of them, fetched water from the river, cleaned the house herself, and acted as a caretaker of the family. Wasu never experienced the burden of responsibilities while Sumi stridden along as the matron.

The seasons in India change regularly bringing every time with them a new climate. Men and women can hardly acclimatise with one before another sets in. The poor are often caught unguarded with their vulnerable bodies and fall prey to deadly diseases. The rich, however, enjoy the nature's changing moods sensing in it the presence of invisible divine power. This discriminating duality on the Indian soil has always been the cause of its degeneration. Wasu had a dreary walk in the scorching heat of the sun when he returned home from his long distanced farm. He was thirsty and wished for a refreshening cold drink. He had entered the village boundaries and approached the well on the way where some women were drawing water. The women honoured his request for water and one of them was about to offer her pitcher to him when someone called out from distance prohibiting her from doing so. "No, no. He is a Mahar and untouchable. He will contaminate our well. Send him away, send him away." The man at a distance yelled at the woman. The woman got alarmed and withdrew. Wasu looked at the man who seemed a familiar face. His throat was parching with thirst and wanted to snatch the pitcher from the woman's hand and drink water himself but he resolved not to do so and return home quietly.

Strange things happened within the next few weeks. A cattleman was beaten up by the upper caste hooligans and a woman's goat gone out to graze in the open did not come back. It transpired later that the animal which had intruded in the crop was caught and killed; its meat feasted upon by the crop owner. Both the cattleman and the woman had approached Wasu with complaints and urged him to find solution to their grievances. The events had turned Wasu introspective who would sit alone for hours and ponder over the happenings. He was not yet able to reach out to conclusions when a ghastlier event occurred. *Hanuman*, the monkey God, is said to be the protector of every village in India and all the villagers worship the idol of the god installed in the temple with great devotion. Wasu's village also had *Hanuman* temple with a huge idol of the God placed in its middle. People worshipped the God regularly and observed fast on every Saturday to please the Almighty. Recently, however, the outstretching courtyard of the temple was used for all other purposes than devotion. When there was marriage in the village the courtyard was used as resting place for the *baratis*. People would accommodate their animals here for lack of cow shed at home. *Truant* boys would play various games in the heat of summer afternoon while their seniors would gamble over rudimentary currencies. All of a sudden, the entire village was caught unaware by stunning news. Wasu was disturbed to hear that someone had smeared the idol of God *Hanuman* with *muck* and the blame had come to the boys of his caste, those who followed him in his newly acquired ideology. The boys were hunted by the police and arrested. They were released after heavy bashing and with a strict warning to remain within their limits. There was a lull in Wasu's *basti* which had been a target of recent atrocities. Wasu himself was puzzled over the series of events that had shaken him within. Such things never occurred before, he was told by the elders, and never were their boys humiliated before. Yes, he had told them, let's see what can be done about it.

Unfortunately, there wasn't really anything Wasu could do about it. His military tactics had no scope to operate here and his personal valour had no direction. The things that happened had no legal support, for they did not fit into the law's stricture. Therefore, Wasu was at a loss to decide a course of action and often lapsed into dejection.

The scorching summer days got over as monsoon arrived. It brought with it new hopes for the poor, for it enlivens agriculture and brings jobs along with it. The entire village folk get busy ploughing land and preparing it for new crops. Then follows sowing that demands a great deal of discerning ability and foresight for the proposed harvest. Practically everyone in the village is involved in the process, and the village, with children attending school, wears a deserting look. Nevertheless, the old and women in rich families stay back home and are occasionally spotted interacting. Even these sights become rare as showers of rain prohibit them from entering the streets.

Wasu had gone to supervise sowing in his field while Sumi stayed back. In fact, Sumi spent most of her time at home, looking after her parents and keeping the house.

Therefore, Wasu left home with usual unconcerned mood and accomplished his work in the field with meticulous perfection. It was dark and drizzling when he returned. He expected his sister to come forward with help to protect him from the shower. However, Sumi did not appear. What he saw was unusual and shocking. Both his parents were at the door in disturbed profile surrounded by women of the neighbourhood. His mother almost began to cry at the sight of Wasu who, by now, had reached the door. "What's the matter?" he asked anxiously while trying to support his mother stand properly.

"Sumi", his mother could utter the name with difficulty. "Sumi has not returned home as yet. She has gone to fetch water from the river when the sunlight gleamed quite brightly. It's more than two hours now."

Wasu smelt something foul but he kept cool. Maybe, he thought, she must have been delayed because of rain, or detained by a friend or acquaintance. He talked to his mother in a pacifying tone–

"Don't worry too much. Sumi will be back soon. She must be on her way home."

"She never takes so long to reach home", his mother told him in a heart rendering voice.

"Wait for a while, I will check," said Wasu and turned back. He called on one of the boys in the *basti* and explained the matter to him. He instructed him further to seek help from others and go in search of Sumi along the river bank. He himself visited friends and acquaintances who knew Sumi well and where she was likely to take shelter while it rained. He returned home to attend to his grieving parents. The old couple refused to relent and insisted upon seeing their daughter in person. Neighbouring men and women had gathered to console them. They all sympathised with the family and wondered why it should happen to the aged couple which was at the fag end of life. Besides, they all revered Wasu and were under his obligation because he had always helped the needy. Time passed on and there was no news of Sumi. The boys had returned without clues and disappointed. No one had noticed Sumi, or any trace of her. No one knew her whereabouts. Rain had gathered force and began to fall with renewed momentum. Darkness grew thicker. Several unpleasant things began to assault Wasu's mind, several disturbing thoughts assailed him. He found himself surrounded by enemies who needed to be annihilated immediately. He had performed those tricks many a time in wars and every time had emerged triumphant. Who are the enemies now, and where are they? He cried out as if he was in the battlefield. He picked a torch and a heavy stick from the corner and came out of the house. The boys followed him. They all headed towards the river which lay covered in the thick darkness of night. They found it difficult to walk as the rain had made ground muddy and slippery. The showers of rain fell down at intervals making the search even more difficult. Wasu called out Sumi's name hoping to awaken her in case she had fallen asleep. They walked a pretty long distance along the river bank and returned as the efforts to locate Sumi turned out futile. All hopes were exhausted and Wasu felt like a soldier caught in deadly trap of the enemy. He sat down and began to cry like a child. Where is my Sumi, where has my dear sister gone? He asked in desperate voice. The boys were moved by the plight of their idol who had appeared a mountain of courage till now. They took him home wading through mud and showers of rain.

The day dawned upon the *Mahar basti* like a nightmare. The news of Sumi's disappearance benumbed everyone. People began to make all sorts of guessing, none of them conclusive. They visited Wasu and his parents to extend sympathy and went away to resume daily routine. Wasu sat alone with his parent planning out the next move. Suddenly, he saw a boy approaching him in hurry. He obviously had news to break. Wasu stood up to receive him and listened to his words. The boy was aghast and unable to speak properly. "Sumi, Sumi," he stammered, "Sumi is dead and lying over there." He stretched his hand in the direction of the river. "Come, follow me," he said and began to run towards the river bank. Wasu followed him in earnest.

Sumi's dead body lay in the mud. Her clothes were torn and smeared with blood. There were scratches on her arms and below the neck. Wasu placed her head on his lap and wiped the face. He could not believe that Sumi was dead and talked to her as if she will respond. He began to wail as reality struck him. The torn clothes, scratches on the body and the blood-smeared thighs revealed that she was raped. He lifted her body, placed it on shoulders and walked towards home. Others, who had assembled at the sight, followed him. His steps moved as if someone pushed him from behind and the movements showed as if he walked in sleep. His parents were almost paralysed with grief and could hardly utter a word when they saw Wasu entering the courtyard with Sumi's dead body on his shoulders. Wasu placed the body on the ground and covered his parents in arms. They had already received the news that made them dumbfounded. They were hardly able to cry as their throats have gone dry and their eyes were wet and swollen. Wasu himself was overwhelmed with grief and did not know how to pacify his parents. The neighbours somehow could control the three and consoled them though their plight seemed beyond consolation.

Wasu realised the need to report the matter to police before Sumi's dead body was buried or cremated. One of the boys wrote down detailed report of the incident and submitted to the police headquarter. Wasu accompanied him to explain the matter in person if necessary. The police registered the complaint with little interest in details and sent them back assuring investigation. The police van arrived in the evening when everyone was tired of waiting. The body was taken for postmortem and returned after a couple of hours. A casual enquiry was made before the police departed. Wasu cremated his sister's dead body with heavy heart and bid her farewell with tearful eyes.

No one knew who the culprit in Sumi's case was; no one could even imagine an enemy to a girl who behaved well with everyone and whom everyone loved. Everyone thought that the social and political antagonism emerged lately between the Mahars and the feudal castes cannot be the cause of Sumi's humiliation and her barbaric death. Wasu, however, thought otherwise. He could visualise the recent changes in social relations and connect the disasters with them. He could ascertain the faces that had dared into the heinous act. He wanted to punish them, eliminate them, if possible and avenge his sister's inhuman demise. But he found himself lonely and helpless. The boys and other helpmates were men without power, without means or assistance. He could lead an attack against the enemy and destroy the perpetrators but this war was different from all the previous ones, for there was no marked enemy here eventhough he knew it by intuition. Therefore, an attack would mean a leap in darkness, a boomerang inviting self destruction. He did not want the boys and others to perish for an uncertain target and a blurred view of the bull's eye.

He decided to wait till the next move by the police which seemed a dimly gleaming ray of hope. That was a long wait, for the police vehicle appeared inside the village after a week's interval. What transpired between the police and the village authority remained in dark leaving Wasu and his boys in wretched desperation. He decided to visit the police station himself and know the progress of the case. Nothing came off the visit. He received the routine reply that the investigation is on and the information will be released as and when due. He returned home hopeless and crestfallen. He had no news to let off, no message to convey. He did not know how to console his ailing parents and his own waning spirit. When the boys and others gathered around him to know, he was speechless.

Monsoon got over and winter came, followed by Diwali. No progress was reported in Sumi's case, no culprits identified. The villagers celebrated Diwali with usual gusto while Wasu suffered in loneliness. The soldier in him seemed to have been defeated.

# 9

# Kulatha Rangan

A feature that distinguishes a woman from her male counterpart is endurance, and Kulatha Rangan had it in abundance. She lived with her parents in a village called Silampatti situated on the sea coast within Madras Presidency of those days. Silampatti was a fishing center which supplied fishes to markets and to other towns in the province. It offered regular employment to a number of families including those who were not fishermen by profession. Kulatha's parents had migrated here in search of job when she was thirteen. They made best of the opportunities and settled down here as a fishing caste. Kulatha was their only child who was brought up with loving care in conditions available to the poor. They went to the sea early in the morning and returned home at the sunset. Cyclones and hurricanes often strike the coastal regions and render life inoperative. They take away the working folk into the deep sea and drown them. Human lives are perished by nature's atrocious moods. Kulatha's parents went to work on a certain day and never returned. She was left alone and destitute. Thus began her ordeal.

Kulatha's parents had left her a house to stay in, four muddy walls with thatched roof. This was a luxury, in view of the fact that there were many homeless wanderers seeking shelter from outrageous climatic changes and to preserve the little earning they make. Therefore, Kulatha had numerous visitors who offered her work and money. Many of them, however, had an eye on her youthful disposition, on her appealing face and figure. She had big broad eyes and straight nose above the curved lips which adored her dark complexioned profile. She could sense while working that men flirted with her, touched the vital parts of her body on pretext of comredarie. She seemed to have enjoyed it though, to realise its nuances later. Many would accompany her to the house and spend time with her talking ceaselessly. Kulatha's innocence and gullibility would never allow her to think of anything serious out of the situation. Her ignorance shattered and illusion fell away when four men raped her inside her own house while it rained outside. She screamed with pain and cried for help, but her voice waned away in the pouring rain and nobody came to her rescue. Her exhausted body lay motionless till she restored strength and woke up to a new realisation.

Kulatha did not go to work the next day. There wasn't really anyone whom she could trust and narrate her sufferings. She found herself lonely for the first time. The workmates and companions were no friends of hers; only a bunch of jesters who would exploit the young girl's weaknesses and laugh at their own jokes. Kulatha's plight did not remain secret. Everyone in Silampatti talked about it blaming the girl herself for what has happened. Women would feel pity and elderly men sneer at her. When she appeared on the work site with her head low and eyes downcast no word of sympathy was uttered, rather a gossiping murmur was heard at large. She felt suffocating amid those men and women and loneliness drove her to the brink of madness. She rushed back home and shut herself inside the house.

No one can remain in isolation for long while hunger and thirst invade the living anatomy. These instincts brought Kulatha out of the house. She had enough money to buy rice and other cooking items. She got them from a shop and prepared meal. She was about to help herself with food when there was a knock at the door. A man appeared within sight. Kulatha recognised him as one of those four men who had abused her ignorance and made it public. He entered the house and sat comfortably on the ground. There was certain calm on his face and concealed determination. He spoke in a calculated manner as he addressed—

"Let's forget the event", he said, "and come to a practical solution. I don't want you to suffer any longer."

"Keep your sympathy to yourself" Kulatha almost screamed at him, "and get yourself out of my house."

"I want you to listen to me and think over what I say. I have an offer to make and it's for your own good," he said looking straight at her.

'No, I won't accept anything from you, the least your pity."Kulatha told him.

"It's not pity, Kulatha," the man said, "It's the penance for my wrongdoing." His genial tone mellowed down Kulatha's anger a little. She decided to hear him speak. The man continued—

"I want to support you from now onwards, to look after you and protect you from the preying eyes of lecherous men."

That sounded good. Therefore, Kulatha allowed him to speak further.

"You will stay here, in your own house. All the amenities will roll at you feet and you can lead a luxurious life. But no one will visit you without my knowledge. I shall spend nights with you, you and me alone, like man and woman..."

Kulatha could realise his profligate intention. The man wanted to keep her as his concubine. Her dark profile started blazing with fury. She showed him the way out and said—

"Away from here, get out of my house immediately and never show your dirty face again."

The man was composed and undisturbed. He made another effort to convince Kulatha who seemed beyond the convincing point. She burst out in tears and requested him to go. The man left quietly.

The food that lay in the plates grew cold. Kulatha found it unpalatable and did not eat. A storm brewed into her mind. It proliferated her miseries and a profound sense of humiliation resulted into depression. She sat down on the ground supporting herself with the wall. She looked ahead of her into a vacuum which reflected nothing and appeared gloomy. She closed her eyes as she felt tired and soon lapsed into slumber.

Kulatha had spent happier days in Silampatti, she had developed fond memories of the place. She was a carefree girl when she had come here, and a darling daughter of her parents. She had wandered in the marketplace and compelled her father to buy red ribbons. She had watched the rising waves of the sea and had basked beneath them. She had observed the sun setting into the ocean and the distant water bidding farewell to him. Men and women seemed so genial and supporting, so unbiased and loving. She loved the village itself and the people therein.

Silampatti now, had become Kulatha's enemy. She wondered why people have turned against her and why she is blamed for the crime others have committed on her. No one called her to work, and, when she herself approached the worksite, no one talked to her. The savings in the house were on decline and soon there will be nothing left. She will have either to starve or to beg, or else give in to the man's demands whose lustful voice frightened her to the bones. Alone in the house, she planned out a move. She was young and able enough to toil and work manually. If Silampatti denies her work, other places cannot be so unkind. She decided to leave the village and go to city. There were several means available to take her to Madras, the place where people are said to obtain jobs easily and where nobody bothers about the past. The thought of unknown future shook her with fear, but her stay at Silampatti seemed more formidable. Next day, she was on the way to the city of Madras.

Madras, during those days, was stirred socially. A social movement had reached every door and young men and women were inspired by the ideals of their leader. The poor and the downtrodden could speak out their grievances which were immediately attended to. Kulatha's fellow traveler took her to a construction site where labourers were in demand. She got an employment along with others, which could help her to sustain herself, temporarily though. The labourers on the site were placed in make-shift accommodation where Kulatha spent her nights with others. She was now a completely metamorphosed person, aware of herself, always on the guard against the misconstrued assumptions of the people around. Nevertheless, she behaved well with everyone, helped the aged and the handicapped, and soon became a part of the surrounding. She would address elderly women as *amma,* who, in return, would show her maternal concern. The young would consider her as their fellow worker who had joined them out of need and never asked her about the roots. She herself seemed to have forgotten it all.

The labourers received their wages at the week end and were free to spend the following day without work. Most of them preferred to rest, while others attended gatherings organised by the activists. Fiery speeches elaborating the miseries of the poor and exposing hypocrisies in tradition would leave the audience spellbound. Glories of the Tamil land and its contribution to the ancient nation would be evoked which would be received with thunderous applaud. The speakers were always educated young men inspired by the towering ideals of the leaders who considered all Tamilians as one community and were bent on annihilating castes among them. They alluded to women as glorious recalling their roles as daughters, wives and mothers and appealed them to join the movement. Consequently, several women had enrolled themselves as activists and participated in agitations that took place regularly.

Kulatha had attended these gatherings on the days when there was no work at hand. She would herself feel inspired while listening to the speakers, and wish, in the heart of her heart, to be a part of the movement. She would hang around while others left when the meetings got over and engage herself in petty works like lifting waste papers, sweeping the ground etc. This had become a regular feature which had come to the notice of the activists who were impressed by her sincerity and a sense of commitment to the cause. On learning that she was alone and homeless, they urged her to join the movement in regular capacity and enhance the proximity of the movement. The movement, as a whole, takes care of its members, she was informed, and she should not worry about her livelihood. Kulatha consented without second thought. She grasped the ideology of the cause and soon found herself busy in permeating its essence.

It was in the midst of activities that Kulatha met Rangan. Thoroughly committed to the movement, Rangan was a young man whose deeds and speeches always matched with each other. He was an effective speaker who could hold the audience in spell for hours together. Being an important member of the movement and a man of thorough integrity, his words and actions were respected by all. He realised Kulatha's urge to be drawn into the group in the first meeting itself. Subsequent meetings brought them closer igniting sparks of love in Rangan's heart for Kulatha whom he found unique. He would watch her every movement, her pleasant profile matched with grace and felicity. He was also drawn towards her buxom appearance which had enkindled a profane desire which always lies latent within the sacred flame of love. Kulatha was taken aback when Rangan proposed her, for she had never thought of herself as deserving for a man like Rangan. The proposal awakened her past, the life at Silampatti, the miseries and wretchedness and all that she had suffered. Her life had been a stigma; a blemish on the God's pure design which cannot be mingled with Rangan's whom she considered as far above the ordinary human beings. To work with him was an exhilarating experience like ozone in suffocating conditions but to ask for it as one's own would be presumptuous. Kulatha tried to avoid the man who had already read her mind's inner working and who, when alone with her, broke the silence—

"I know I cannot give you much in life, for I have spent all that I had for the movement, but I shall certainly try to keep you happy within our limited sources. Please accept my proposal and be my better half so that we can work together with renewed zeal and enthusiasm."

Kukatha did not know how to respond. She wanted to tell him that she is not worthy of his love, that her past life had been a muck and ...but she was silenced by Rangan's further beseeching whose earnest voice left her speechless. Rangan took her hand into his and kissed it with due politeness. Kulatha had no courage to resist.

The marriage was not a big affair. Kulatha got married with Rangan in a simple ceremony attended by a few. Since both of them were dedicated workers and committed to the movement, their union came as a pleasant surprise to all. Everyone considered it as a good sign and a step forward to a casteless society which was one of the cherished goals of the movement. Kulatha was no longer a single person, but had doubled, and her name came to be written down as Kulatha Rangan. She had found a new identity and her life seemed to have found a new direction as well. She loved her husband, who, in return, showered all his sentiments on her as a man and companion. They spent most of their time in the movement and, when alone, in each other's arms. Kulatha looked for better days ahead.

The past, however, followed her secretly and caught her up unaware. Rangan had brought home a man with him who knew Kulatha. He was a fisherman from Silampatti who led the workers on the sea and brought them back. He paid the workers their wages and knew each one of them by name. He somehow got associated with the movement and became one of Rangan's trusted pals. He recognised Kulatha instantly but pretended to be ignorant. When he left home with Rangan, Kulatha grew anxious and the Silampatti days appeared before her eyes like heinous serpents.

Rangan returned home late that night. He wore strange looks. His face seemed to have been distorted with anger. Kulatha's heart sank at the sight of her husband. She went to him with usual frankness but he avoided her and went to the study. Kulatha approached him while he turned away. "What's wrong", she asked.

Now he looked at her and said—"Nothing, except deception in love."

"What does that mean?" She asked imploringly.

"Don't try to be innocent", He raised his voice and asked her further—"Do you know the man who had come home today with me?"

"Yes", she said. "I think he is from the place where I lived earlier, the place called Silampatti."

"Good. What else do you remember about the place?" He asked looking straight into her eyes.

"What else? Nothing remarkable." She told him.

"You liar. How do you forget your prostitution at Silampatti, your flirtation and the men with whom you slept regularly?" His voice trembled with rage.

"No, that's not true," she said. "That's not the truth." She experienced a sort of helplessness while she spoke.

"What is the truth, then, and why did you conceal it from me when I proposed you?"He roared at her.

"I, I tried to reveal it to you on several occasions, but you never allowed me to..." Her voice choked with grief and she fell down at his feet. Rangan was furious as he considered this another trick of the woman. He almost pushed her away with the feet. He was in deep grief himself as he felt deceived and maneuvered. He moved away into the corner and cried like a kid. Kulatha raised herself and tried to console him. That infuriated him further. He turned violently against her and slapped on the face. Kulatha reeled away in pain. He held her by the hair and dragged out of the house. He then returned inside and shut the door against her.

It was dark outside and cold. The stars gleamed away into the sky as if to mock at Kulatha's plight. The noise of insects and the occasional barking of dogs were heard, and an owl's hooting away somewhere added horror to the scene. Kulatha turned back and looked at the house. She had spent happy hours and enjoyed the bliss of marriage inside it. Suddenly, it had turned hostile. Where shall she go now, alone—no, she realised, she was no longer alone—but carrying Rangan's child in her womb for more than three months. She thought of reminding Rangan of that, but she decided not to, for Rangan would not think of it as a suitable reason to let her in. She moved away in the dark like a sleepwalker knowing not its destination.

The movement ran into full swing and Rangan's role in it fully applauded, Kulatha's missing presence, however, was never felt. She was lost like a drop of water in the ocean.

# 10

# Confessions of a Graveyard Keeper

They called me *Amarendra* because, while I attended to the dead, entertained the living. Then someone explained to me the meaning of *Amarendra*—the God *Indra* who is immortal. I was amused. I was amused because immortality had descended onto me from heaven though for namesake. That encouraged me to work with more enthusiasm, dispose of the dead human bodies either by cremating, or by burying them in the ground. My father called me *Bhutya*, the ghost king. Maybe that was my real name, I do not know. But I know the date of my birth very well, the month, year etc. because it coincided with the death of Nehru, the man who ruled India once. Yes, ruled, because, I was told, he was an unequivocal decision maker who was never questioned by his colleagues. They followed his instructions like good school boys. Well, I do not know much about it, so better leave it. My birth coincided with Nehru's death because, I was told, while my father was busy arranging Nehru's pyre, my mother experienced labour pain and I was born soon after. How long had it been now? How many years? Forty eight? That determines my age. I am forty eight years old.

My parents were sent to their original place after the nation mourned the death of its first prime minister. We came down to

Varanasi, the ancient *Kashi*, where my father took up a job of attending the dead on bank of the river Ganga. He was the king *Harischandra* and my mother *Taramati* cremating the dead bodies on the river bank, while me, the prince *Rohidas*, their only son, crying for food when beset with hunger. The dead would come to my help when hungry. I would steal food left on the pyre by the mourners, obviously for the departed ones, and pacify the basic instinct without my parents' knowledge. I discovered that this was an easy way to obtain food, for dead bodies were cremated everyday and the last rites performed regularly which included feeding the dead. Nobody knew that a living boy was fed on the food left for the dead ones till my mother suspected absence of greed at the time of our regular meals. I behaved like a matured adult refusing to eat more and asking my parents to consume. That was unlike of me who had always been crying for food reminding my parents continuously that I was born hungry. My mother smelled something foul and decided to discover it. After a cremation got over and the mourners went away I found my way to the burning pyre. I picked up food left by the side and went behind the rock to eat as usual. My mother followed me. She caught me eating and then drinking the river water. She picked my ears and warned me against indulging in any such act in future.

We were on the Ganga *ghats* nearly for fifteen years. I grew up along the Ganga *ghats* listening to the mantras chanted by the *sadhus* and wailing of the mourners who performed last rites for the dead. People from across the river villages were ferried to Varanasi and back home. Young boys swam along the boats and helped the passengers reach safely to the shore. It was a lovely sight and I watched it for hours together. At times, I experienced an overwhelming desire to swim across the river, or be a boatman at least, hardly aware of the fact that a boatman needs either a boat of his own, or money enough to hire one. My heart would sink in dejection with the realisation that I had none. Nevertheless, I had learnt swimming with the help of local boys, all of them from the *chandal* community staying around the *ghats* in tents or huts. Some of these had reached adolescence and took delight in watching women who religiously dipped into Ganga leaving their breasts uncovered knowingly or unknowingly. The boys talked about the women openly amid roaring laughter and amusement. It was here, in the holy water of Ganga, that I experienced my first erection. It was here, again, behind the rocks and bushes, on the bank of *Gangamai*, that I had my first successful masturbation.

My father died unexpectedly leaving us dazed and bewildered. He died of snakebite. As he was drawing wooden logs from the heap to place them on the pyre, a deadly serpent appeared from somewhere and stung my father who was rendered lifeless instantly. His death had caused inconvenience to those who had hired him to attend to their dead. They hired another keeper who was asked to clear the place of my father's dead body. He held my father by leg, dragged him into the river, and pushed the body into the main stream. *Gangamai* engulfed him immediately, while we, my mother and me, tried to locate him on the surface of the water, with eyes running short of tears.

My mother was compelled to leave Varanasi *ghats*, for the sight of a widow was considered inauspicious there, and was not allowed to operate in any capacity. We moved away to a place called Rampur where a large graveyard laid waiting for us. Rampur was a small town sparsely populated but the only place to bury the dead, or cremate them for the villages around. Therefore, when funeral processions reached there, several at a time, Rampur assumed the looks of a pilgrimage, invoking the holy mantras and witnessing a variety of flowers hurled across the dead bodies. It appeared a busy town, temporarily though. We had raised a small hut beside the graveyard to stay in and soon found ourselves busy helping the mourners who would willingly pay us for the assistance rendered. An official graveyard keeper of Rampur, an old man of about eighty, objected to our presence but soon gave in to my mother's youthful charm with the hope, perhaps, that the woman, someday, would give in to his passions' scepter, dangling lifelessly bellow the distorted belly. He allowed us more space, and helped us to transform the hut into a four walled muddy house. That became our permanent shelter, a place to be my home for the rest of life. This man, known in the locality as Anda Bhurji, would visit our place quite often, particularly when my mother was alone at home. If, by chance, I happened to be present, he would send me away on some pretext or the other. I hated his approaches but could do little about it as my mother was pressed under his obligation and seemed to be assured of his ineffectively hanging garden.

When Anda Bhurji died he was denied a place in the graveyard, for it was preserved exclusively for the higher castes. He, being a *chandal*, was considered as an outcaste. When his relatives tried to bury his dead body in a corner of the place, the efforts were thwarted. The body was thrown out in the Ganga, and the compassionate mother of Deovrut, swallowed it ungrudgingly. Anda Bhurji who had spent his lifetime in keeping the graveyard, took utmost care to maintain the place properly, was thrown out of it when dead...

*Karmany akarma yah pasyed*
*Akarmani ca karma yah*
*Sa buddhman manusyesu*
*sa yuktah krtsnakarmakrt*

My mother wept bitterly when Anda Bhurji died, not because she loved him, but probably because she was used to his untimely appearances and his breathless panting when he moved around her like the rooster that flirts a hen. She suggested a permanent tie-up with his family and convinced me to marry one of his daughters, the youngest who was almost of my age and as dark as tar. This girl had a giggling habit who would twitter like a sparrow even in serious situations. When my mother closed us in a room at the night of wedding she was giggling all the time and then everything ended up in a big silence.

My mother had withdrawn herself from work as she found it more tiring and stayed back home while I worked with my wife on the graveyard. I had become the sole authority on managing affairs in the graveyard as no one from Anda Bhurji's family had come forward to stake the claim. Of course, his daughter, whom he seemed to have drawn up from a coal mine, was now my better half and a constant companion. She was a total contrast to me in appearance, for I had taken on my father, fair and tall, while she, a dwarf walking in a night smeared with darkness. People had always appreciated our match, nevertheless, because we were dedicated workers and offered full assistance to the living and to the dead. And, of course, we were always together, a reverse version of Radha and Krishna, working in unison till the dead were vanished from the sight and the living departed.

A graveyard is supposed to be a place where the dead are either buried or cremated. A belief prevails among the people that it is populated with ghosts. The living fears the place and shuns it at large. That is a misconception. A graveyard has always been a safer place to those who have nowhere else to go, for those who are discarded by their own kinsfolk. I had myself protected a young couple which had eloped and married against its parents' will. I remember the story so vividly—

Rampur had a mixed population. People of all castes among the Hindus and a sizable Muslim community formed the population of the town. They all lived happily together. The Muslims, who had inherited feudal titles and wealth from their ancestors, hired the poor Hindus for domestic work. A young Hindu boy called Janam worked as domestic help to Nawab Khaliluddin who ran a small business of selling funeral items to both the Hindu and Muslim communities. Janam had an easy access to the Nawab's house and could interact with the women. A trusted servant in the house, Janam often took liberty to mix up with girls who otherwise were protected from strangers and outsiders. No one ever suspected his involvement with Zamzam, the youngest daughter of the Nawab, who fell in love with the robust and handsome looking Janam. The affair was finally discovered by elderly women in the house who immediately reported it to the Nawab. Janam was sacked from the job and was threatened with dire consequences if he was seen around the corner. Zamzam's young heart craved for her lover as she was deprived of his sight and was compelled to remain in *hijab*. She somehow was able to smuggle out a letter to Janam asking him to meet in the graveyard at night from where they could steer forth towards the next goal. I found the two figures moving in the darkness and asked them to stop, for I knew that the dead do not move around in the graveyard in the night, the living do. I also knew that only the wretched on the earth come to the graveyard while living, others sneer at it. I instinctively understood that the intruders in the graveyard need my assistance and asked them to approach my house at the other end. Janam had met me on a couple of occasions earlier and knew I stayed there. He rushed with his beloved into my house and spent a few hours together. I advised the two to swim across the Ganga before the daybreak and reach to a safer place, which they agreed to. My wife wished the couple happy future as it disappeared in the twilight.

It was a matter of shame for the Nawab to realise that his daughter had eloped with a Hindu boy who had been a servant in the family. He hushed the event but only for sometimes. Its revelation shattered him. He committed suicide by taking an overdose of sleeping pills. I had watched the funeral passing by as the Nawab was being taken to be buried in the graveyard marked exclusively for the Muslims. I wished I could bury the man and his discomfort with him.

I had to visit Rampur on various missions. Procuring of wood for cremation was one such job which often took me to the town. Since the wood was brought to the town from remote forests, a long wait at the site was always inevitable. Sometimes, I had to spend long dreary hours in the nearby temple which was almost in ruins. I was waiting as usual for the cart carrying the wood when I heard bustling noise behind me in a corner. As I looked back, I spotted a man and a woman engaged in the act of mating; the man moving rhythmically to and fro, and the woman screaming with ecstatic pleasure. I watched the couple and felt myself roused. I even felt my manhood in the pocket, but feared the consequences of witnessing the act and left the place in hurry.

My mother, who had now lapsed into old age, was often sick. She was well taken care of and attended to by us but her sickness stayed on like an unwelcome guest who would not go. I had planned to admit her in the government hospital where the poor are treated free of cost but she had no desire to leave the graveyard which for her was the home. My earnings were barely enough to cover daily meals and left no scope to treat her privately. She died when we were away attending a pyre. I was overwhelmed with insurmountable grief, for my mother's death marked the end of my childhood, it had ceased much earlier though.

I knew that the graveyard where my mother worked and shed her perspiration was not meant for her dead body. I also knew that the place which otherwise was in my sole possession, was not my property. Whose property was it then, I mused. It belongs to the dead who transcend all the worldly barriers, all the manmade reservations of castes and creeds. Why, then, my mother who had been an outcaste while living, should be the same after death. The thought of taking her corpse away somewhere and, possibly throw it in the muffled water of *Gangamai* repelled me enormously. I decided to bury her within the graveyard itself. I confided the plan to my wife, who, barring the complexion, was bright in all other demeanors. We waited for the nightfall and, when darkness became thick, dug a pit large enough to accommodate my mother's dead body. We laid it into the pit quietly and covered with the mud. We made the spot plain avoiding the mound so that no one could suspect it of a grave.

Years have passed since then. My mother is lying peacefully in the pit, and I am as busy as ever. My wife has lost two of her front teeth; therefore, she avoids opening the mouth and observes silence as much as possible. My chattering mynah rarely sings these days.

# Index

R



S



T



U



V



W



Z